GET OUT OF MY HEAD

Discover Practical Was To Get Rid of Negative Thoughts and Focus
On The Voice Of God

CONI KNEPPER

Pumzika Press

Contents

Cover design and illustrations by Get Your Book Illustrations
Paperback ISBN- 978-1-7357164-5-9
Hardback ISBN- 978-1-7357164-6-6

Knepper, Coni
Get Out Of My Head/ Coni Knepper
Get Out of My Head is a book for those looking for help in how to take control of their thoughts
by knowing the difference between God's voice, their self-talk, the enemy's lies, and the
pressures of this world. Learn ten practical hands-on methods of learning to listen to God.

Get Out Of My Head
Is dedicated to my loving husband who walked with me and never gave up searching for answers to the voices tormenting my mind.
Without his input, patience, and love for Jesus this book would not be possible.
I love you, Harold.
oxxoxo

What people Are Saying After Reading Get Out Of My Head

"If you are having trouble with the negativity this is the book you need to read. This amazing author has captured my voice in book form. When speaking to people in the world its ALWAYS been hard for me to hear God. Even without hearing Him I still kept my faith. Within chapter 1 I was hearing from God. Once the voices within my head were separated and labeled my ears were opened completely. Just with chapter one. Continuing through the book it became evident that God worked through Mrs. Coni Knepper to write the guidelines to get closer with God. Not only could this book will help a 40 yr old but it would be a youth teaching tool. For the first time in my life in one practical experiment, I heard the applause of the trees. That night I found the verse to support this wonder. Isaiah 55:12. This one lil nature walk became my crazier faith in God... Thank you, Coni I am so glad you wrote God's heart. It has helped 2 people in my life so far. God works through what you at least except. I thank God for being able to read and experience this book."

—Bonnie

"WOW! Amazing 'experiments' to hear God's voice. I've read Coni's children's books and loved them, so decided to get this one, too, and I'm so glad I did. Several years ago I learned to recognize the sources of the different voices in my head - self, satan, peers/family, or God — but this author does a fantastic job explaining what it means to take every thought captive, to recognize when those thoughts are based in fear or pride, and how to hear God's voice. She offers ten techniques or experiments that truly put you in touch with the right side of the brain, making it easier for God's voice to be heard loud and clear. I highly recommend this book. These experiments are incredible."

—Tina

"Literally changing my life. The first word I'm going to say is WOW. I'll be honest, I was a little nervous going in, didn't really know what to expect, as have never really read any sort of "self-help book before, but figured "yeah ok, I'll give it a try..." Man, have I been VERY pleasantly surprised!

A bit amazing, a bit almost creepy in a way, how someone who's never even met me could write something and be saying things so spot-on, so perfect, so... like they were written just for me, like she's talking directly to me!

Yes I know I've had some issues, have had a lot of doubts, negative thoughts, have felt quite... lost and confused for so long I've almost gotten used to it. But maybe I didn't know or didn't realize, just how bad it was until reading this... hearing these things and most of all having to be faced with and admit to myself all of the thoughts and feelings that have been packed inside for so long, some that have never been said out loud...

I love how she refers to things we do in our everyday lives and inter-twines them with thoughts/conversations with God, and easily explains ways to put into practice such simple, yet important and effective actions (ie positive thinking, stopping, and asking where thoughts are coming from, praying throughout the day, both for good and bad. I LOVE the Think About What You Think About segment!).

...I have already been finding my head being much clearer, negative thoughts so much fewer, and so seldom that I can recognize myself stopping them, talk/pray myself thru, and turn it around. Still so new that has to be a conscious effort sometimes, am not gonna lie. I'll be totally honest—still absolutely shocks me how much of a difference these things—which before I started seemed so huge and impossible, but now seem so simple—are already making, so that's what keeps me going at it, knowing how much the littlest things can do, seeing and feeling how much better I am even already!"

—Jessica

Introduction

Get Out Of My Head offers clarity and direction by identifying how to know the voice of God. The Author of your very being is requesting *you*, allow Him to draw you into His presence.

Do you have conflicting internal voices battling for your attention? Are you unclear on how to detect the conflict between your voice and God's? If you're a new believer, you may struggle with why you continue doing things you don't want to do. You might think, *Why do I feel depressed? My life is okay.* Imagine your mind being clear of conflicting thoughts, free from chaos. Envision living the abundant life God sees for you. Do you want that?

Perhaps Jesus is your Savior. You desire a jump start or innovative ideas to differentiate between self-talk and God's instructions. This book will cover that, even including evaluation questions to aid you in determining what prevents you from hearing God's voice.

Each chapter presents a unique approach to listening to God with step-by-step directions on how to engage with God within the specific section. I urge you to complete one practical experiment a day for ten days. Then, work backward and choose your favorites. If you come upon an exercise you're not sure you will enjoy, no worries, try it and see; you may find a hidden gem.

Over the last thirty-plus years, I have led teens and adults through these practical activities to hear God speak. Stories of students experiencing encouragement, direction for themselves, and growth in their relationship with Jesus are limitless. Trust me—listening to God is not wacky hocus-pocus, and poof, God speaks to you. It takes effort, but your time practicing these teachings produces the positive benefits of life-changing results.

TESTIMONIES

Here are two cases of adults whose lives changed after training in listening and hearing God's voice.

 My takeaway from participating in the *Get Out Of My Head* activities is the quiet times. Every morning, Harold and Coni gave us Scriptures to meditate on while having time connecting with Jesus. We sat still or walked around as long as the first person we communicated with was Jesus Himself, no one else. Something they taught us was to download our thoughts, which makes listening much more effective. To this day, I teach my youth group and my children how to download and listen to God. I remember the activities giving me time to connect with God and myself, which helps me teach youth today. I am constantly thinking about how I can continue to build in Listening to God moments.

—Jonathan Coates—Children's Pastor in Ellensburg, Washington.

 The biggest impact of learning to hear God's voice was listening. As a teenager, I wanted to be the one talking and telling, but intentionally being still and listening was new information. After learning the practical activities on how to hear God through developing listening skills, now I crave times with Jesus and me. I trust God to put on my heart daily things He asks me to obey. I can trust His voice.

—Kelly Collins—wife and mother of three in Lodi, California.

Before you dive in, here are some initial instructions:

1. If you are not clear on your relationship with Jesus, please read Chapter 16 before continuing any further. If you have received Jesus as your Lord and Savior, awesome!
2. If you desire to be open to discovering God in a fresh way, then don't hold back on listening to God or you won't experience His presence. Jesus will not impose Himself on you. #1 and #2 need to be in place before moving forward to the Practical Experiments.

My "voices" story started thirty-five years ago when I discovered freedom from depression, suicidal thoughts, and confusion by learning whose voice I was listening to.

Why I needed to write about "voices"

The rain beat on my windshield as I pushed through puddles, splashing gusts of spray across the hood of the van. The wipers could scarcely keep up with the pounding of hail and wind. My knuckles turned white as I clutched the wheel; tears covered my cheeks. I headed towards the church to meet with Dr. Neil Anderson. My husband set up an appointment to meet with Neil to discuss the voices in my mind. The image of sharing with another expert in "freedom" made me want to vomit. How could this appointment be any different or of benefit? *Just drive over the center divider of the freeway.* The words kept echoing in my head. Or a deeply familiar voice: *You are no good and stupid.* I should crank the wheel and drive through the center divide.

"Get out of my head!" I screamed. Suddenly, I found myself stalled in the church's parking lot outside the door where my appointment with Mr. Anderson was to take place.

Neil greeted me and gestured for me to take a seat for our "Freedom Conversation." With a groan, I barked out orders on how there was no way I was going to have any discussion with him or the older couple sitting in the room's corner.

Neil shook his head and smiled. I let everyone in the room know what I thought of them and their *freedom.* The voices grew stronger, demanding that

I leave and run away. My initial preference was to race back to the van and hurt myself, but something prompted me into the room. The atmosphere seemed different. Why do these people wish to listen to my story? A lonely love seat invited me as I plopped myself into one cushion. I conceded to stay for a bit and no longer.

Two and a half hours of identifying how my past and Satan had seized control of my life was exhausting, even though I felt exhilarated. During the appointment, my prayers filled the room with sobs as my mind was set free from a lifetime of lies. There were no heads spinning, casting out of demons, or green goo coming out of my mouth. My appointment with Neil was a time of freedom, not an exorcism. Neil then proposed I go to the restroom and wash my face.

I will never forget this moment. As I leaned over the sink with cupped hands full of sparkling clean water, I splashed the handfuls of refreshment over my entire face. Looking up into the mirror, I gasped. *I'm not frightened to look at myself,* came from inside me. The evil faces of death vanished. I couldn't get out of the bathroom fast enough. I needed to tell someone. "Neil," I shrieked, "I like what I see. I like ME!"

Neil laughed and added, "Yes, that is why I suggested you wash your face."

"You tricked me," I said chuckling, and suddenly I stopped. "Listen," I said, "the voices of torment—they're gone. For the first time in my life, my mind is still and quiet. I am FREE!"

Years of studying how to hear God's voice, being trained in Freedom In Christ appointments, and remaining free became my passion. My life has consisted of taking children, teenagers, and adults through the same freedom prayers I experienced. God prepared the *Practical Experiments* my husband and I developed over the last thirty-five years. There is no greater joy than watching people set free from sins and destructive lifestyles.

Each activity encompasses the whole range of inexperienced to long-time believers. Whether negative thoughts rule your mind or you have an occasional struggle of spiritual uncertainty, depression, or even anger, the experiments will help you to hear God's voice. Maybe you crave connection with

God and to develop a deeper walk with Him. I promise doing these activities will usher you into a deeper walk with your Savior, Jesus.

There are many excellent books composed by notable Bible scholars teaching how God loves you. I can tell you—God loves you. He will never leave you, and He wants to speak to you and show you incredible things, but until you experience listening to the voice of God, you will never believe me.

Heck, I was a pastor's wife with three children living the life of church ministry, instructing people on how God cares for them; however, I was not free myself. Different voices ruled my heart to the extent of wanting to give up on my marriage, children, and life. I needed to learn how to hear God's instructions and know which voices tugged for my attention.

Hearing the voice of God is not just for missionaries in Africa, pastors of megachurches, or Billy Graham himself. It is for *EVERYONE*. Jesus died for all of us, Jews, Gentiles, men, and women, which means Jesus communicates to everyone who will listen.

Get Out of My Head is an easy read with simple how-to directions. It is for new believers and seasoned followers of Christ. Exciting activities provide a process for you to take notice of the Great I Am, Jesus Himself.

Now, let's dig in!

ONE

Who Are These Voices?

YOU ARE in charge of your mind and heart.

This chapter comprises a list of specific voices begging for your attention and how you can take control of each one. They want to rule your mind. Until you recognize that they are real voices fighting for control of your life, and challenging the abundant life God has for you, your freedom will continue to be smothered in darkness.

As a child of God, Jesus gives you the capability through His Holy Spirit to hear *Him*. He is not withholding from you, waiting to pop out with an audible surprise: *"Here I Am!"* Yes, God speaks audibly, but this book explains hearing God daily, not as a once in a lifetime experience.

The 4 Voices In Your Head

MY VOICE

Self-talk is continuing minute by minute. If you are not mindful, self-rambling can contribute to destructive behavior or apathy. Daydreaming and putting off responsibilities are signs of self-talk getting the best of you. Thoughts like *I'm not good enough; I can't do that*, or *I wish I could* _____ *(fill in the blank)* can quickly turn into depression or self pity parties. You can wish and wait for years before anything happens if self-talk is not controlled by God. Listening to the One who knows all your hopes and what is best for every situation leads to beneficial self-talk.

Self-talk can be helpful; it depends on what you are thinking about while talking to yourself. Is it a conversation that brings peace, joy, excitement, obedience, along with thinking of others? Or is it about selfish desires? Is it full of worry and stress?

World noise creeps into our self-talk through the media. These sources cause feelings of loneliness and sadness. We can talk ourselves right into depression if we are not careful, which can lead to blocks between you and God's voice. He doesn't stop talking; you stop listening.

THINK **about what you think about.** Sounds silly but it's true.

Take a minute and turn to Chapter 17 at the end of this book. Find the Philippians 4:8 poster.

Read through each word slowly and carefully.

Spend sixty seconds — GO!

How do you feel? Was it difficult to concentrate on what is right, lovely, pure, etc.? Did you find it easy or unsettling? If thinking about God's Word is a foreign concept, no worries, it takes practice. The Holy Spirit helps you if you ask. The *Get Out Of My Head* activities will help you recognize when the Holy Spirit is calling you to listen. Filling your mind with God's insights, instead of worry and selfish thoughts, opens up your spiritual ears to hear God's instructions for your life.

God gave us His Word to think on, to meditate on.

> "This book of the law shall not depart from your mouth, but
> you shall meditate on it day and night, so that you may be
> careful to do according to all that is written in it; for then
> you will make your way prosperous, and then you will
> have success." —Joshua 1:8

This idea of meditating on God's Word is to help you hear Him, and it comes with a promise! You will prosper and be successful. That doesn't mean you will become rich and famous in the world's definition. It means you will hear God, grow closer to Him, have endurance during hard times, love others, with an ongoing list of benefits. Yes, there are rich and famous believers; however, the scriptures are clear that being successful is *knowing God*, not acquiring stuff. Hearing Him is top of the list of success.

When you know God, all other things in this world fade away.

> "The world is passing away, and also its lusts; but the one who
> does the will of God lives forever." —1 John 2:17

It pleases God when you listen to Him. As a child of God, do you want to please Him?

If we draw near to God, He *WILL* draw near to us.

> "Draw near to God and He will draw near to you."
> —James 4:8a

God is not sitting on His throne looking down on you; He is near you and has treasures to share with only you. You are His treasure, His child; why wouldn't He want to talk with you? That's how special you are.

However, your self-talk can convince you differently if you allow it. Maybe it's difficult to connect with Jesus because your mind is full of many other things, and not God.

In this next section you have the opportunity to examine your self-talk. What are words or thoughts you tell yourself? It's time to be honest; no one else sees your checklists. It's between you and Jesus.

Taking Control Of My Voice

This is a checklist of lies you may have believed over the years. Circle the ones that apply to you. Then pray and ask God for any other lies you may have been speaking to yourself. Write them out at the bottom of this list.

- I have no time for myself.
- I'm not good enough and never will be.
- If I ask for help, people will not want to be around me.
- I'm a terrible mom, dad, wife, husband, person.
- Any drama at work or school is my fault.
- My spouse is cheating on me *OR* I want to cheat on my spouse.
- My work doesn't matter. No one appreciates me.
- I am exhausted, worn out, but that's what makes me good.
- I wish I lived somewhere else, with someone else.
- If only I had _____ then I would be happy.
- Shopping will make me feel good.
- I wish I looked like that woman/man.
- Why doesn't anyone like me?
- I hate myself.
- I'm ugly and fat.
- No one will ever want me.
- I hate my life.
- Life is too painful.
- When I complete this _____ then I can rest.
- Resting is not for me! I can't stop. If I do, people won't love me.
- Life doesn't matter anymore.
- I am stupid.
- If only people would listen to me and do what I say.
- I know better than he/she does.
- I'm going to burst inside!
- I'm more valuable when I stop talking.
- Get out of my head! I feel like I am going crazy.
- I can't let my children/grandchildren fail, or people will assume I am an awful parent.
- Look how happy our family is. People want to be me.
- I'm terrified it won't work, it's too hard, it's too expensive. (The *too* syndrome)
- I don't need to go to church or stream a service.
- Prayer never works for me.
- I can read my Bible tomorrow or on Sunday. I don't need it right now.

- If God cares for me, then why do bad things keep happening?
- I have sinned so often. God will never forgive me.
- I watch porn to benefit my relationships.

Write Out Three of Your Self-Talk Messages

1.

2.

3.

Next

1. Review the statements you circled that apply to you.

These are blocks between you and Jesus. Count them. Each one is a lie representing a barrier or wall, causing silence in hearing God speak. God has not stopped listening or speaking to you. Your poor life choices cloud your mind and the ability to hear spiritual directions while turning your focus away from listening to what God has for you.

Statements like, "I can't hear God" or "My prayers just bounce off the walls" happen when negative, prideful, lying self-talk creep into your thoughts making it impossible to hear God communicating with you. He does not stop loving you, but He does allow you to choose what you think about and what goes into your mind.

Are you struggling to resolve something in your life and you can't figure it out? You're not sure what to do next? Imagine all of the blocks you checked off actually towering between you and God. This is a wall of lies cemented between you and God, but HOPE wins. You can get rid of these blocks and hear the voice of God.

. . .

2. One by one, share your self-talk struggles out loud with Jesus. Then physically lift your hands and surrender them to Him. Confess and repent to Jesus.

> "If we confess our sins, He is faithful and just to forgive us our
> sins, and to cleanse us from all unrighteousness."
> —1 John 1:9

Confessing to God and repenting means you make the decision to stop thinking about whatever is causing the blocks between you and Him. It is beneficial for you to confess these sins out loud. Thinking them in your head leaves room for a quick noncommittal conversation instead of a real confession. In later chapters a more detailed reason why you should speak out loud is explained. At this point, trust me—out loud is powerful.

Jesus already knows you think about these things; confessing to Him is not for your salvation, it's for your relationship with Christ, so that you can hear His voice in everyday situations.

God promises to forgive all your sins if you confess to Him, including the self-talk areas separating you and Jesus. It's the first step towards hearing the voice of God and having a vital relationship with your Savior.

He loves you and will never quit caring for you. I realize everyone says this, however, you are about to experience it personally.

3. Now, the fun part. Ask Jesus to replace those ideas with thoughts that bring you joy, hope, fun, and love. You pick.

People usually forget this part, leaving their minds open to disappointment. Confess to Jesus and tell Him you are sorry for thinking about those things, then ask Him to REPLACE them with great ideas. Ask Jesus to give you BIG ideas. If you are serious about hearing God speak to you and long to do great things with God as His child, then this is an important step.

Checklist of BIG IDEAS!

Read and circle the ones you want Jesus to help you maintain as daily thoughts. Jesus wants to bless you. You are His child and He cares about what you think about in your self-talk.

- I am going to _____ today.
- Jesus loves me every day.
- Jesus died for all my sins.
- I am going to share the Good News with someone today.
- Before I choose TV/social media, I am asking God what He thinks I should watch.
- As hard as today is, I know you are here with me, Jesus.
- I am a child of God: forgiven, holy, loved, different from the world.
- I have the same power living in me that lives in Jesus. His spirit, the Holy Spirit.
- I can do anything God asks of me.
- My children/grandchildren matter to God; I give them to You, Jesus.
- I give You my spouse and choose to love him/her even when they are not lovable. (*I am not talking about staying in an abusive relationship.*)
- When stress and worry come into my mind, I choose to give them back to You, Jesus.
- I will find an accountability partner with whom to share my self-talk struggles, and vice versa.
- When self-talk comes into my mind against the plans God has for me, because it will, I will tell it to go to Hell where it belongs. I have authority as a child of the King.
- THIS IS NOT SOMETHING I AGREE TO THINK ABOUT. I DO NOT GIVE THIS THOUGHT PERMISSION TO SPEAK TO ME!
- Add any other Big Ideas God brings to your mind by recording them in a journal.

Now, don't freak out. I am not suggesting we can assign *people* to Hell. I *am* saying to look at your self-talk and how it makes you feel about yourself and others. Does it match the Word of God? Yes? Great! If not, you can send those thoughts to Hell, because you have the authority as a child of God almighty! As a follower of Christ Jesus, this is our fighter verse. This is a familiar verse for some people, but look again, there is power in belonging to God.

> "To all who received Jesus, to those who believed in His
> name, He gave the right, (some translations say power) to
> become children of God." —John 1:12

You belong to a family with a Father who loves you more than you can imagine. You possess the same Spirit that lives in Jesus Christ. Think about that. Sending a thought to Hell is no big deal for a child of God.

Get rid of your negative self-talk when it seeks to come back. Decide *NO, I am a child of God, a treasure to Him, and I choose not to agree with this kind of self-talk.* Jesus will help you. Just ask.

THIS IS NOT SOMETHING I AGREE TO THINK ABOUT.

I DO NOT GIVE THIS THOUGHT PERMISSION TO SPEAK TO ME!

Hang these words up on your wall where you can see them to remind you of the power God has given you to overcome negative self-talk. You are no longer a victim of your circumstances, but a warrior that is feared by the enemy or anyone who tries to mess with your mind.

When I first started taking control of my self-talk, I replaced thoughts at least 100 times a day until it turned into a habit. I know precisely when my self-talk is about to take over and lead me down the depression and anger road. I can choose to spiral into destructive thoughts or confess them to Jesus and ask Him to replace those thoughts with Scripture or big ideas.

In the scriptures, it's known as taking every thought captive, before they get into your heart and become a part of who you are.

"We demolish arguments and every pretension that sets itself
   up against the knowledge of God, and we take captive
   every thought to make it obedient to Christ."
—2 Corinthians 10:5

"As a man thinks, so he is." —Proverbs 23:7

This can seem strange to a new believer, but my hope is as you continue reading *Get Out Of My Head*, you will have a better understanding and tools on how to take control of your mind.

Example

It's easy for me to fall into the busy-writing-and-emailing-people trap. Hours fly by and then I have a thought: *Ask Me*. God wants to be part of my every moment. God is a part of my books. He and I write them together; however, I frequently allow my own voice to take over, doing the work in my strength. A racing, anxious feeling comes over me alerting that I need to surrender my self-talk and obey Jesus. Once I do this my writings flow and the anxious thoughts leave.

The voices inside of us are not always evil thoughts. Sometimes they are busy being ME thoughts without regard to what God thinks. I ask Jesus for big ideas all the time. Suppose my self-talk takes me back to past mistakes where I feel bad about myself or others. I stop! I replace those negative thoughts with the BIG IDEAS. Once you do this for a few days (it does take practice) you will see your thoughts are encouraging, positive, and GOD'S VOICE. This is not a positive thinking exercise, it is dependence on God to replace the negative thoughts and He will. None of us can do this on our own strength. We need Jesus giving us the desire to want to change our self-talk. Ask Him for the desire and see the change from rambling self-talk to Holy awareness.

"…for it is God who works in you to will and to act in order to
   fulfill his good purpose." —Philippians 2:13

The next voice you hear in your head is the one that never fails, gives up, or stops loving you. I pray you will recognize this voice and allow it to guide your feelings and choices in life.

God's Voice

It's a still small voice resonating in your heart or mind. It can be an impression, idea, or thought that brings encouragement. It's the voice that says you belong to Jesus. It never invokes the feelings of fear, anxiety, or shame. It's always the feeling of hope, full of mercies or start-overs as I like to call them. Each morning, God gives you a new day to do His will with His help. Your past is behind you!

Whenever a thought comes, such as you are kind, you are unique, you have a purpose, I made you because I love you— thoughts urging you to come back to Him when you have sinned—these are from God Himself.

You hear His voice in His Word, the Bible, from trusted believers, and within your heart.

In future spiritual experiments you will learn to hear God's voice from the Bible.

As a follower of Jesus Christ you have the Holy Spirit living in your soul, your very being. He is prompting you to think and do good things. The Holy Spirit urges you to confess, repent, and then gives you assurance of forgiveness and cleansing. His voice brings comfort, encouragement, and strong faith, which is how you know the thoughts are from God and not the enemy, Satan.

Notice I said "followers of Jesus Christ" and not "believers." Even Satan believes in Jesus, but he is not a follower of God's Words. I believe in Jesus Christ as the Son of God who died for my sins. Because of what Jesus did for me, I choose to follow His Words in the Bible. Can you say the same?

You cannot be good enough to think of positive things consistently on your own; however, you can do all things with Christ's help.

"I can do all this through him who gives me strength."
 —*Philippians 4:13*

You are able, with the power of God's Holy Spirit, to think and share the Good News of Jesus Christ. These are responsibilities for all believers.

What?

Now, wait a minute. I'm not a missionary like you! Well, you are. Missionaries, Christians, Christ's followers, believers—these are titles for anyone living a life for Jesus as their Lord. One does not hold a greater responsibility than the other. The desire to share the love of Jesus happens wherever you live. It doesn't have to be in Africa.

God has plans for you to prosper and do great things for Him (Jeremiah 29:11). Prosperity doesn't mean you will be rich. It means you will go forward in what God has planned for you. When you get to Heaven, as promised by God, you will hear Him say: "Well done, you listened to my voice and obeyed." It is never too late to hear God's voice.

Example

As I shared earlier, teaching these Practical Experiences to children and teens over the years has been my passion, something God has now allowed me to share with you adults. Thank you for taking the time to read *Get Out Of My Head*. I promise you will not be disappointed if you trust God and obey what He shares with you during the experiments.

Two of our eight grandchildren are at the age of understanding these concepts. While visiting, I tried some activities with two of my grand girls. Kylie at the time was ten, and Karis, her sister, eight. We began decorating their room with posters and an enormous paper title across one wall: HEARING GOD'S VOICE.

The girls cut the letters out and hung them perfectly from the ceiling. Later, behind the words, they displayed the ten different *Get Out Of My Head* Practical Experiments that you will learn in future chapters. After two weeks of rising early in the morning and doing one of these listening experiments, Karis found she longed to do them, even after I returned to Africa. The time

I spent with Kyle and Karis came about through listening to the prompting of the Holy Spirit, believing young children can hear His voice, and then asking for a Big idea.

God is faithful when we ask for more of Him and creative ways we can be used to reach others for His glory. I love change and prompting people to experience God in ways they never thought possible. Being with the girls and witnessing their spiritual growth was a gift from God; all I had to do was listen and obey.

Testimony- Karis

 My bedroom looks great! Seeing the words—Hearing God's Voice—as I wake up, it really helps me not give into temptation to go do my day without listening to God first. I highly recommend decorating with your own experiments and posters. My favorite *Practical Experiments* are *Nature* and *Love Letters*. *Nature*, because when I am outside, I can see all the things God created, and I feel close to Him. *Love Letters* because God speaks right to my heart, and it helps me feel loved, especially on hard school days. I keep His letters to me in my journal.

Karis is nine years old and already miles ahead of adults I know because she refuses to give in to the lies Satan throws at her. She struggles much like all nine year olds, but she knows how to listen to the voice of God that brings her hope.

Sure, it's hard to get going early in the morning, but who put that in your mind? "I can't spare 30 minutes (or any minutes)." Again, who is whispering these lies?

The next voice that blocks you from hearing God's voice is the deceiver. The one who hates you and wants to see you fail and yet we give him permission to enter our thoughts daily.

The Enemy's Voice

Satan's voice is accusing, nagging, and mocking. It generates fear, confusion and rejection, and can even create doubt about what is right and wrong. The devil brings a blanketing, choking, general sense of guilt and shame as though everything is wrong and there is no clear action you can take to remedy the problem. A sense of weakness and hopelessness can result. His desire is to deceive you by weaseling his way into your head and heart. Feelings of past sins or abuse cause you to believe you will never be forgiven. LIES! He sends messages that you are unloved, discouragement, and even hatred towards yourself.

Then, if he can't make you bad, he will make you busy. Overflowing schedules, long to-do lists, and flat out ignoring time with God are all ways the enemy steals time away from hearing Jesus speak. Some people in this world think that if they don't believe Satan exists, then he doesn't. People used to think the world was flat. Did that make it flat? Nope!

Whether you are fully aware of it or not, Satan is your enemy. He opposes God and all of God's people. He is behind every evil thought entering your mind. Satan desperately wants you to listen to him and destroy God's kingdom.

He is a fallen angel who hates YOU. He plans to destroy you and your mind.

> "Be alert and of sober mind. Your enemy the devil prowls
> around like a roaring lion looking for someone to devour.
> Resist him, standing firm in your faith, because you know
> that the family of believers throughout the world is under-
> going the same kind of sufferings." —1 Peter 5:8-9

Don't stop reading; there is more to the story. God kicked Satan out of Heaven because Satan thought he could be God. He wasn't willing to obey God's voice. Rebellion and pride separated him from God.

> "How you have fallen from heaven, morning star, son of the
> dawn! You have been cast down to the earth you who

once laid low the nations." —Isaiah 14:12 (Satan is
referred to as the morning star)

Today, the enemy puts thoughts into your mind to make you think you can do all things without God. However, the opposite is true. Satan will never whisper the truth into your mind, only lies.

Satan is the father of lies, which is how you can be sure when you hear lies in your mind that they are not from God, but Satan.

> "Satan is a murderer from the beginning, and does not stand
> in the truth, because there is no truth in him. When he lies
> he speaks out of his own character, for he is a liar and the
> father of lies." —John 8:44

Have you ever texted someone or involved yourself in something that didn't seem right, but you went ahead with the idea anyway? Where do you think the temptation came from? God doesn't tempt.

These thoughts tickle your ears.

It's just a little lie; no one will know. Regardless, it will make everyone happy if I don't tell the entire truth.

> When tempted, no one should say, "God is tempting me." For
> God cannot be tempted by evil, nor does he tempt anyone;
> but each person is tempted when they are dragged away
> by their own evil desire and enticed. Then, after desire has
> conceived, it gives birth to sin; and sin, when it is full-
> grown, gives birth to death. —James 1:13-15

The lie enters your mind and you push it aside. The thought comes back; however, you allow it to fester. Then you ask yourself, what would it look like to carry out the idea? You take the step; you follow the lustful lies and BOOM! Feelings of guilt and shame flood your mind.

Or, no one sees you do it, but the shame inside is like a horrible secret. As secrets hide in your mind, they move to your heart, and turn into depression, anger, fear, fighting with people, unforgiveness, and many other feelings. It all starts with a thought.

Where do these dangerous thoughts come from? From the enemy! Satan and his followers, which are demons. There is nothing to be afraid of because you are a child of God and the Holy Spirit lives IN YOU.

> "Do you not know your body is the temple of the Holy Spirit
>   within you, who is from God?"
> —1 Corinthians 6:19

This means you are powerful and can crush any thoughts the enemy has against you.

But how? In the next few chapters, you will experience power from listening to God. God is working *in* you and giving you the capability to stand up against Satan and his demons.

Think of a flea on the floor. The bug hops all over the place; he even bites you. It itches annoyingly, but the flea can't take over your life. What can you do? Step on him! Stomp him out. Jesus died and rose again to give you the same power against the enemy. Satan wants you to believe you are weak and afraid, but it's not true. You are powerful, a giant compared to demons and their plans. They have already lost the fight. When Jesus died on the cross for your sins, Jesus also conquered Satan and his demons for you.

Satan is a fallen angel; he has powers, but he does not have the same powers as God. He can only be in one place at a time, whereas God is everywhere. If Satan can only be in one place, do you think he would choose *you*? I'm sorry, but you and I are just not that big of a deal for Satan. My guess is that he's after prominent people to cause bigger messes. However, he has one-third of the angels from Heaven working for him. They don't know you personally, but they know what weakens Christ-followers. They can submit notions in your mind, which prompts disobedience and feeling discouraged about yourself. Here is the point: Satan and his workers/demons only have power if you give it to them.

Wait a minute!

There are two ways to provide the enemy a place and power in your mind:

1. Through *sin*: Actions/thoughts you chose against God's Word, which is why you need to know His Word so you can see Satan's tricks and temptations.
2. Destructive self-talk: Every time your self-talk is against God's Word, you are saying, "Welcome, demons, to messing me up." They have NO power unless you hand it over to them.

Satan's intentions are to stop you from informing others about Jesus and cause you to feel defeated. His helper demons are searching for a way into your mind. Remember the lion roaming around watching for someone to devour? Satan can not take away the promise of your salvation, but he can cause you to be ineffective if *you allow him*. See, you are the boss of him. You are the owner of what you think about and how you handle your thoughts. People do not realize this while passing through life, fumbling over thoughts and ending up depressed, asking, "Why?"

If you choose to listen to the voices in your head saying you are worthless, stupid, your life doesn't count, etc., then you will believe the lies from the enemy and miss out on the life God has for you. No matter your age, God has an abundant life where He and you can conquer anything together.

So, how does the enemy put these thoughts into my mind? I love Jesus and go to church; I read my Bible sometimes and even pray at night. What's the deal?

Good questions. Bad habits of listening to negative lies can be broken if you take an honest look at how you have been deceived.

Checklist of Ways the Enemy Can Deceive Me

1. Pray for God's help and guidance in bringing up whatever ways you have been deceived.
2. Read through the list below and add any others that come to mind.
3. Circle any actions and narratives that may have had a part in your life. Be honest with yourself.

- I can do anything on my own. I don't need anyone (Isaiah 41:10).
- I can listen to or watch anything. It won't affect me. (Google — 10 negative ways social media affects your brain. We wonder why our minds are full of internal struggles.)
- I don't need to attend/listen to church services because the people there are hypocrites *or* because I have better things to do (Hebrews 10:25).
- My kid's activities are much more important than church. They could earn a scholarship (Matthew 6:19-21).
- The Bible is old fashioned and out of date (Hebrews 4:12).
- My neighbors are an irritation. Let the pastor tell them about Jesus (Matthew 16:15).
- If I share the Good News, people will laugh at me or dislike me (Luke 9:26).
- I am an introvert and don't like people (1 Peter 2:9).
- I am an extrovert and have all the answers people need (Proverbs 16:18).
- The worship at my church is out of date (Ephesians 5:25-27).
- The preaching at my church is boring. (Pray for your pastor and watch your attitude change.)
- It's only an innocent lunch date, my spouse doesn't need to know (Galatians 6:7-8).
- Just keep quiet. Your ideas don't matter (1 John 4:8,16).
- The government owes me; I am not paying all these extra taxes (Matthew 22:21).
- It's only a little lie; no one will know, and it doesn't harm anybody (Proverbs 12:22).
- Why don't I ever get a break? People who are not believers live better than I do (Psalms 73).
- I'm never going to get a job. God doesn't care about me (Luke 12:6-7).
- I will never forgive that person for what they did to hurt me (Colossians 3:13).
- No one can tell me what to do. I'm old and set in my ways (Titus 2:3-5).
- Add any other deceptive thoughts you need to be free from.

NOW WHAT?

Confess each area that you have given your mind over to the enemy.

Replace it with what God says is true.

Example #1:

It's only a little lie; no one will know, and it doesn't hurt anyone.

 Lord Jesus, I have lied to _____ about _____. I now know it hurts our relationship. I choose to repent of this lie and replace it with the truth.

The truth is _____. Psalm 145:18 says, "The Lord is near to all who call on him, to all who call on him in truth." I cry out to you, Lord, wipe away this lie and allow me to make this lie right with _____.

Example #2:

If I share the Good News, people will laugh at me or hate me.

The enemy can't take away your salvation and he will make certain you don't share the Good News with anyone else.

The world should hate you because you are not of the world.

> "If the world hates you, keep in mind that it hated me first."
> —John 15:18

They even rejected Jesus, and yet He commands us to go into all the world and share the love of God with everyone. Life is short. I would rather have someone hate me for following Christ than love me for joining them in lies.

Lord Jesus, forgive me for not caring about the lost in this world. I choose to share how much you love them. I pray for

_____ and _____'s salvation. Use me, however you wish to reach them for you. I choose to set aside my wants to help others know You.

Using the examples, go through each area where you have given the deceiver permission into your mind. Pray for forgiveness and then confess your sins to Jesus Christ the lover of your soul. Replace each lie with the truth from God's Word. You can look up the verses provided after each statement, google Scriptures, look them up in your Bible, or ask a friend for Scriptures that match your particular deceiver thoughts. Skipping this part will leave a huge open door for the enemy to re-enter your thought-life, which blocks hearing God's voice.

It is difficult, but I promise you will receive a blessing from the Lord. He is ecstatic to reveal Himself to you in His Word.

When you come humbly to God, He lifts you up.

> "Humble yourselves before the Lord, and He will lift you up."
> —James 4:10

These thoughts are ways the enemy takes control of your mind. Remember, you are the boss of what passes into your thoughts, not Satan nor his follow-ers, *you* alone. Every time you choose to believe the lies on the checklist, it hands over permission for the enemy to walk right in and plant seeds of doubt about who you are: fears, loneliness, disobedience—the list goes on. If Satan can lead you away from God, he will. He is a thief, while God gives life.

> "The thief comes only to steal and kill and destroy; I have
> come that they may have life, and have it to the full."
> —John 10:10

Satan and his servants can not possess you as a believer, but they can cause you to be ineffective as a follower of Christ when you allow them to take over your thoughts. When you allow Satan permission into your mind, you become depressed and wonder why, or rage out of control and abandon loved ones.

The "Golden Rule" is to love others the way you wish to receive love.

> "For in everything, do to others what you would have them do
> to you, for this sums up the Law and the Prophets."
> —Matthew 7:12

It protects all entrances for demons to enter your thoughts. If we love each other and ourselves, our thoughts will remain close to God and far from the enemy. Where there is love, Satan and demons can not survive. When we sing out praises or statements of faith in the name of Jesus, Satan flees, taking his companions with him. Do you see the power you have?

Example From My Own Life

I come from a family of liars struggling to acknowledge the truth. There is continuous stress and abuse, to the point that my family has stopped talking to each other. They believed the lies about one another and provided the enemy what he wants—the destruction of a family.

Because of the decision to not allow Satan into our minds, my mother, siblings, and I can have open conversations about Jesus. It's a daily choice to love them. I wanted to be furious at my family and join the hate train, but God advised me that I needed to be different for the sake of their salvation.

Today, my siblings, mom, and grandfather claim Jesus as their Lord and Savior.

My mind is clear to hear Jesus when He says, "Love them as I have loved you." Who am I to hold back love by not forgiving someone when Christ's forgiveness for me is endless?

Years ago, my husband and I learned this and decided our family would be different, and it is. Our three children follow Jesus and know how to hear the voice of God versus Satan's voice seeking to deceive them.

When attacks from the enemy come, and they will, you need to know the techniques of cutting off his plans against you. Knowing who you are in Christ gives you the power to overcome and ward off attacks. Taking stock of who you listen to and what you allow in your mind blocks any ways in which the enemy can enter your thoughts.

But there are also other voices people listen to and follow, sometimes without any regards to whether it's harmful in hearing God speak. These come from friends and peers.

Friends and Peers

It matters who your closest friends are.

> "Do not be misled; bad company corrupts good character."
> —1 Corinthians 15:33

I am not saying to care only about people with the same beliefs as you. We are to love everyone, but our closest friends need to be people who we can trust won't speak lies into our thoughts.

> "The righteous choose their friends carefully, but the way of
> the wicked leads them astray." —Proverbs 12:26

Not everything people say to you is accurate. Not everything you see on social media is true. Yikes, don't get me going there.

> God warns you to protect your mind.
> (—Proverbs 4:23, Colossians 3:2)

When agreeing with a lie, you swing open the door for sadness, pride, arrogance, and selfishness, just to name a few. Do you fight with your friends all the time? Is there constant "drama," gossip, and slander in your group of friends? Maybe someone is not honest. Perhaps there is jealousy or hatred in the group. Do the people you choose to spend time with speak poorly of their spouses? Whatever it is, you need to identify and repent of it and replace it with God's plans. Remember, if you don't ask Jesus to replace the views of your companions, misery and drama will continue, and no one will be happy. Worse yet, God's plans for you to hear His voice are futile.

Taking time to think about your friendships and how they affect your thought life is a good habit to develop at any age.

Friendship Checklist

Ask God to reveal the truth about your friends and peers. Then circle the statements that match the definition of your friendships.

MY CLOSEST FRIENDS:

- Do not believe in Jesus Christ as their Savior.
- Do not believe in the church as the bride of Christ.
- Do not believe Jesus is the Son of God.
- Enjoy teasing with slander and gossip.
- Lie and exaggerate often.
- Do not read God's Word.
- Think I have a crutch in believing in Jesus Christ/God.
- Refuse to talk about spiritual things with me.
- Have no control over their anger, swearing, and hateful remarks.
- They are good people, but have no interest in God.
- I constantly have to be happy to show them that being a Christian is fun.

Your friends may match none of these statements, which is excellent. If the closest friends in your life fall under this group, you need to confess to Jesus and ask for some new friends. Don't abandon your friends, but do join a group of followers to be real with and seek advice on reaching your lost friends.

Again, if your friends cannot encourage you in your walk with Christ, your ability to hear God turns into rambling self-talk.

You learned about the four voices that can take control of your thoughts and lead to emotional problems along with unanswered prayers and a frustrated relationship with Jesus Christ. Hopefully you took each section seriously and went through house cleaning in your mind.

By now you should be able to recognize when your self-talk is being negative, the enemy is trying to trip you up, you need new best friends to encourage each other. God's voice should be getting easier to hear.

Go back and count the circled statements. Remember these were walls between you and hearing God's voice. How many did you break down? How does it feel to be free from the lies you were listening to about yourself? GREAT!

In the next chapters you will score yourself on what attitudes are stopping your ability to hear God and obey Him. When you complete these first chapters and start the practical experiments your mind will be ready to receive all the wonderful treasures God wants to share with only you.

Hang in there; you can do this!

TWO

Wait a Minute; I'm the Boss

It would be easy after reading chapter 1 to respond, "The devil made me do it," or "I can't change who I am. Everyone talks bad about people." These are lies from Hell, by the way.

Again, the enemy and your self-talk can lead you towards the road of destruction where the ability to hear the voice of God is unattainable. Your choice.

In chapter 1, we covered the different voices controlling your thoughts when you allow them.

Along with voices, there are four central attitudes in life that block hearing the voice of God daily.

Take a few minutes to read through these statements. Circle the ones that most describe you and then score yourself to determine which areas you might struggle with in hearing God's voice. You need to be honest with yourself and add any additional statements that come to mind.

1. I don't need friends, especially those prone to telling me their opinion.
2. I have a fear of dying.

3. I can watch whatever I want on TV or social media; it doesn't affect me.
4. A little lie won't hurt anything.
5. Sometimes I feel sad and don't know why.
6. If someone hurts me I will verbally attack them.
7. I am often more concerned about controlling others than developing self-control.
8. I do not need anyone.
9. I am afraid of failure.
10. When someone hurts me, I stop talking to them.
11. Shopping and redecorating my home are top priorities for me. I deserve it.
12. I do not enjoy reading the Bible; it's boring.
13. I don't like to pray; it's a waste of time.
14. I have worked hard for my possessions; I don't have money to tithe.
15. If my children do not obey, I will look like a terrible parent.
16. I am not good at patience.
17. My job has to come first or my family can not live the way we like.
18. Speeding on the freeway or hiding info on my taxes is fine.
19. If someone talks badly about me, I have the right to tell other people.
20. There is nothing wrong with lying to my family to keep the peace.
21. There are members in my family I hate. God can deal with them.
22. My boss is a pain. I disagree with most of the things he/she does.
23. I have a strong desire to do my will. Rarely do I ask God for His opinion.
24. The world is a scary place and I choose to not be a part of it anymore.
25. I have degrees/achievements that give me the right to tell others what to do.
26. I'm afraid of losing my salvation.
27. Most of the time I hate the way I look and feel.
28. I have no formal education, which is why I am stupid.

SCORING **Yourself**

If you circled mainly these numbers: 1, 2, 5, 6, 8, 9, 10, 11, 13, 14, 17, 19, 20, 25, 26—

Selfishness is causing you to think more about your issues instead of concerning yourself with what God prefers to say to you.

IF YOU CIRCLED MAINLY these numbers: 1, 2, 3, 4, 5, 9, 12, 13, 14, 18, 20, 22, 24, 26—

Disobedience/Rebellion is putting blocks between you and hearing God's voice. This can lead to becoming a person who is difficult to live or work with along with not hearing God speak.

IF YOU CIRCLED MAINLY these numbers: 2, 5, 6, 9, 10, 14, 15, 19, 21, 24, 26, 27, 28—

There is some **unforgiveness** in your life causing you to not hear God's voice. Letting go of the painful memories and allowing God to heal you will open up avenues in your mind to hear God in ways you never imagined.

IF YOU CIRCLED MAINLY these numbers: 1, 2, 3, 5, 7, 8, 9, 11, 14, 15, 16, 17, 18, 19, 22, 23, 24, 25, 26—

These are **pride** issues that you'll need to work on in order to hear God's voice over your own. Pride is the killer. It's a trust and control issue. It means daily deciding to trust people and allow others to make decisions, along with trusting that God knows best for your life. You can't hear God speaking if you don't trust Him.

SELFISHNESS, disobedience, unforgiveness, and **pride** are four key areas in life that block hearing God's voice and understanding His Word. To score yourself accurately you need to count all of the statements you circled and see which areas scored the highest. If two or three areas scored close, then count both as ones you need to work on to be able to hear God clearly.

Let's look at each area.

SELFISH ACTS

When your thoughts and actions are about what you demand, no matter how others think, you are operating from selfishness. Much like a two-year-old. Spend time with a toddler. They grab things that are not theirs, cry when they don't get their way, and need someone to teach them simple life skills. Children under six years old are the picture of selfishness—we learned to be selfless, but somehow selfish desires creep in without noticing. They replace the voice of God in our minds.

Selfishness is turning your back on God while trying to live life without listening to Him. Selfish people admit that they have no need for God, which is what the enemy wants them to consider. This lifestyle leads to greed, dissatisfaction, sadness, confusion, and depression. How can selfish people hear God? Think about what you think about.

There are life-changing things you can do to replace selfishness. These clean your mind to achieve the most from the practical experiments.

FOR THE NEXT **60 seconds be still and listen.**

You will need a pen and paper for this exercise.

- Ask God to show you where you are thinking of yourself over others.
- Next, write whatever comes to mind. Just write words with no concern about good penmanship, spelling, or grammar. It's not a writing exercise.

Once you have completed the first part of the exercise, continue below.

- Look at the items you noted. Circle pronouns I, ME, MY.
- Do you see a pattern? "I want this," "I don't appreciate listening to

other people," "I have plans and no one is going to change my mind," "Everyone else is wrong."

- When you are the center of your thoughts, it becomes difficult to hear God's plans.
- How can you change these thoughts into spiritually productive self-talk?
- Ask God to help you remove the selfish concerns in your mind and replace them with *HIS* thoughts.

Example

While writing this chapter, I kept getting interrupted. I had a plan; I wanted to finish this chapter today. I needed to write 2,000 words and I didn't want disturbances. It was *my* plan.

One of our staff went to the hospital to have a baby, a teacher at our primary school gave their letter of resignation, leaving a classroom without a teacher and, since it's Monday, the weekly staff meeting is at our home. *TODAY!*

The selfish part of my thoughts said, "Let someone else take care of these problems." Typing that sentence makes me gag. I put writing over people I love. This is a wake-up call.

My day went this way instead:

On the way home from picking up the new baby, I stopped and purchased some much-needed fruit for the mama. Then I drove over to the primary school and met with the principal to encourage him. Two primary school teachers arrived for interviews replacing the teachers who resigned. The staff meeting went smoothly, ending early, and here I am typing chapter 2 feeling positive about the day and knowing God used me to speak to others.

Sure, I could have remained at home and written my precious 2,000 words, but I would have missed hearing God say, "Go; *MY* plans, not yours." We miss out on discovering God's voice and serving others when we choose self-ishness.

Unfortunately, I know of several other times where I did not listen to the Holy Spirit's tug and missed out on what God had for me.

. . .

YOUR TURN

Take three minutes and record your selfish story. Be honest with yourself. Recall a day when you did what you wanted without asking God His opinion. Or a memory where you did your own thing and then changed your mind and followed through with God's plan for your day.

After writing *MY SELFISH DAY*, ask God to forgive you and replace the selfish acts with His plans and His power to change. You can't, and I can't, act in love when selfish attitudes flood our minds.

Ask God to grant you the desire to do His will and for spiritual ears to hear the Holy Spirit, then the power to obey. The Holy Spirit lives *in* you, which means you have the strength. Every time selfish thoughts enter your mind, grab them, confess them, and then replace them with God's ways.

Selfish attitudes also lead to disobedience and rebellion against God. If you scored high in the selfish area, most likely your score in disobedience and rebellion are high as well.

DISOBEDIENCE/REBELLION

When you stand against any person in authority over you, including God Himself, and demand what you want, it's the same as witchcraft.

> "But Samuel replied: 'Does the Lord delight in burnt offerings
> and sacrifices as much as in obeying the Lord? To obey is
> better than sacrifice, and to heed is better than the fat of
> rams. For rebellion is like the sin of witchcraft, and arro-
> gance like the evil of idolatry. Because you have rejected
> the word of the Lord, he has rejected you as king.'" —*1
> Samuel 15:22-23*

Disobedience invites the enemy and shuts off your spiritual ears to hear God's voice. This kind of attitude leads to a mind full of misery and confusion.

As an adult, you may assume you are not obligated to obey anyone. NOT TRUE!

God is your Heavenly Father and has rules to protect you. When you disobey His Word, traffic laws, or people in authority over you, what happens? Pride or shame and anger build up, causing self-hatred, leading to outbursts, depression, and lies in your mind. You may end up losing your job or a friend, or paying speeding tickets. This is exactly what the enemy wants.

You are a child of the KING, King Jesus! You are holy, a saint, loved; no one can separate you from the love of God. It's exciting to realize God thinks highly of you.

FOR THE NEXT **60 seconds be still and listen.**

A paper and pen/pencil are all you need.

- Ask God, "Where have I been disobedient or rebellious?" Sit and listen as thoughts come to mind and record them on paper. It can be a list of words with broken sentences; these are for your eyes only.

Once you have completed the first part of the exercise continue below.

- Now, look at the words or phrases you wrote. Where do you need to change your thoughts?
- Confess them to God and ask for forgiveness. New Mercies (Psalm 31:22).
- Ask God to take these disobedient actions away from you and exchange them for kindness, love, obedience, patience, and whatever God whispers to you while praying.
- Listening is the key to this exercise. Take longer than sixty seconds to let the Holy Spirit clean house in all of the circumstances when you were disobedient to God's instructions.

Here is the big question. Do you want to be free from disobedience and rebellion? Do you want to be well?

In John 5 Jesus is at the pool called Bethesda. There are a great number of people with disabilities lying by the pool, hoping to be the first person to get into the water when it is stirred. Hoping to be healed. Jesus sees an invalid that had been laying there for thirty-eight years and asks the man, "Do you want to get well?"

Sound strange? But the man's reply is much like ours today. He says in John 5:7, "I have no one to help me into the pool when the water is stirred. While I am trying to get in, someone goes down instead of me." Excuses and blaming are what the man says to Jesus. We make up reasons for why we can't change or believe it won't work for us like it does for other people.

Imagine people living a life of rebellion and disobedience with no desire to change. They would rather not hear God's voice than change their lives. Instead, they choose to live with fear, depression, shame, guilt, sicknesses, and pride over hearing God encourage them with His truths. It is their identity yet they live with sickness in their minds.

Because you asked God to bring to the surface ways you are rebellious and disobedient, He shared a list of items with you. The list you wrote is from God Himself. They are attitudes causing difficulties in hearing the voice of God and His guidance. You are the boss! Ask yourself: Do I want to hear God or continue in what is equal to witchcraft? Believing these experiments won't bring you hope in knowing God's voice is a lie. I will ask again,

Do you want to be well?

Example

In the morning, my husband and I read God's Word, play worship music, and enjoy the first hour of the day in the presence of God. We no longer have children living in our home, making it easy to start our day in quiet. Hang in there, parents and teachers, your day will come.

My husband never misses a morning. He looks forward to his time with Jesus. They discuss the plans for our non-profit organization and life.

I tend to jump out of bed, ready to GO! Moving into a sit-and-be-still time is challenging for me, but when I obey God speaks memorable verses to my heart and mind.

Time with Jesus can remain in silence or taking a stroll outside. There is no wrong way to listen to God. It's common to find me dancing around, raising my hands, and praying for our kids, grandchildren, and ministries. God gave us our personalities to enjoy Him.

When choosing to hurry out the door and skip time with Jesus, rebellion and disobedience sneak into the day's choices. Those are the times anger flares up and patience with others is short.

God has told me on countless occasions, "Come be with Me. I love you; I want to tell you wonderful things." Why do I disobey when I know it hurts Him and my relationship with Him? The answer is the ugliness of rebellion and disobedience, thinking I can do my day with a morsel of memorized prayer and swish out the door.

When we choose to disobey, we welcome our old self and the enemy to waltz right into our minds, leading the way to destruction. Bottom line, I can't be good, patient, kind, and have self-control without time with Jesus first. It is His presence that gives me the power to obey His voice and big ideas.

When we first moved to Africa (coming up on twenty years ago), our friends thought we were crazy. Leaving a strong ministry, friends, family, our grown children, and moving halfway around the world with no plans except to love others first? Crazy!

We could have said no to God. He'd still love us. We can't lose His love, but we could have missed His best plan for our lives by disobeying the authority of His voice speaking to us.

Life in Africa has not been easy. I miss our children and grandchildren, but I also wouldn't wish to live anywhere else. My days are full of sharing the Good News of Jesus Christ with people who want to learn the Gospel's truth. And I know I will live eternally with our children.

Thank you, Jesus, for FaceTime and Zoom calls!

There is another difficult area in our lives that can cripple us. It brings back haunting memories we all want to forget.

UNFORGIVENESS

Here is the big one, the reason you can't hear the voice of God daily.

Forgiving others is a much harder act to follow through with. Unforgiveness is in your heart where no one else can see except you and God. You can put on airs that you care while actually entertaining harmful thoughts in your mind with certain people. A fake smile or a "How's it going?" sounds good, but if inside you want to punch them, it's probably unforgiveness. It eats holes in your stomach, brings up nightmares, breaks up families, causes other illnesses like chronic depression and even suicidal thoughts. Who do you think is laughing now?

Yes, Satan and his demons. They can not touch your salvation, but they can make you so miserable that your life no longer plays out the plans of God. Especially hearing God's guidance. The Holy Spirit is nudging you to come and be with Him, but unforgiveness haunts you, bringing shame and guilt as your best friends.

So, what do you do? You need more than a 60-second timeout to ask God. Think about people in your life who have hurt you, stabbed you in the back, forgotten about your feelings, or left you alone to suffer silently—no matter how long it has been.

Are you thinking, "Man, this is serious." It *is* serious! The enemy wants to destroy you. Remember the flea? That's all he is unless *you give* him the authority to take control of your mind through unforgiveness, selfishness, and disobedience.

> "For if you forgive other people when they sin against you,
>   your heavenly Father will also forgive you."
> —Matthew 6:14

Ask yourself—How is my sin any better than the person I need to forgive?

. . .

NOT JUST 60 SECONDS–LISTEN, **Obey, and Get Rid of The Pain of Unforgiveness**

You need a pen and more than one piece of paper.

- Ask God to reveal to your mind people who hurt you. You may need to sit still for a few minutes. Let the Holy Spirit bring up circumstances, pain, and unforgiveness trapped within you. As names come to mind, write them down on paper. Don't ask yourself why; just write. Give yourself a few minutes to compile the list. My first list consisted of over 30 people I needed to forgive, and several from whom I needed to ask forgiveness.

Once you have completed the first part of the exercise, continue below.

- Next is the challenging part, but I know you can do this with the help of the Holy Spirit to carry you through each name. It's okay to ask for God's guidance.
- Look at each name individually and speak out the truth of how they hurt you. What did they do? How did it make you feel? Again, out loud, allowing yourself to feel the pain. You have been stuffing these events in your life too long. It's time to give them over to Jesus and be FREE!
- Then speak out loud: "I choose to forgive this person today because I need to be free to hear God's voice and no longer feel awful about what they did to me."

You are choosing to forgive them for *yourself*. You do not agree with their actions nor are you letting them off the hook with God. He can handle them. You are not even saying that how they treated you is okay. No, you are taking them out of your heart and giving them to God. You can even lift your hand with their name inside and physically say, "Here, God, take them; I don't want to feel this pain anymore." It's an act of trusting God that He will take care of them. Whoever hurt you will have to answer to God. God can do whatever He wants to make sure you are free.

You might get to a name that especially challenges you. You may need a more extended period of time forgiving; that's fine. Go back to their name later and finish forgiving them. Forgiving is not a feeling it is an action—a choice you make on your own to bring wholeness to your mind, which in turn means hearing God daily.

During your forgiveness time be bold, speak out loud, yell if you need to, let the tears come, but don't stop until you have told God all the hurt and memories. This is not a time to say I will forgive this person later because it won't happen. You are deciding to forgive to bring healing for *you*, not them. After you have forgiven a name cross it off and move onto the next name God brought to your mind.

IF *YOU* HAVE OFFENDED someone and need to forgive yourself, then speak that out. Tell God you are sorry for bullying someone, lying to a friend, hurting your family with your words, or anything that comes to mind. God is leading this, so let Him stir things up in you.

The next part of unforgiveness is asking God to fill you with a love like His for people. WOW! Imagine asking God to show you how to love people the way He does. His desire is for you to seek Him, but be ready for a life you never thought possible.

This is not a one-time exercise. Forgiving others is a daily routine. You need to start a habit of letting go of offenses as soon as they happen. Hurts are real, but you can control them and give the hurts to Jesus.

When you have finished forgiving the people in your life who've hurt you, believe me, you will feel like a ton of bricks have been lifted off your chest and shoulders. It's worth the tears and pain to let the memories go. When they try to come back, cut them off again with forgiveness. It's common for the enemy to try and convince you that you did not really forgive the people on your list. Or your self-talk may whisper lies that you can't really forgive that person for abusing you. It's true, you can't on your own, but with God you can. He wouldn't ask you to do something and then leave you alone. God is with you giving you the strength to forgive others as He has forgiven you.

It can be tempting to skip over preparing for the next attitude that blocks hearing God's voice, but don't do it! Read on.

Pride

God hates pride because it's self-centered instead of God-centered.

> "Let not the wise boast of their wisdom or the strong boast of their strength or the rich boast of their riches, but let the one who boasts boast about this: That they have the understanding to know me, that I am the Lord, whole exercises kindness, justice, and righteousness on earth for these I delight, declares the Lord." —Jeremiah 9:23-24

God never hates *YOU*. He despises what pride and selfishness do *to* you. He desires for us to know and understand Him. Remember the plan of the enemy? Kill and destroy—pride is the ringleader in keeping you from hearing God's voice.

60 SECONDS–LISTEN **and Obey**

- You need pen and paper and an attitude of humility.
- Ask God to bring to your mind any and all ways you have been prideful towards others and yourself. As you write prideful statements ask God to replace these prideful actions and thoughts with His grace and mercy towards others.
- If nothing comes to mind then ask again. We all have prideful thoughts. We have fallen from the original plan and taken a bite of the apple because we thought we could be like God. Pride started in the garden with the first man and woman, and it has only grown worse as individuals grow farther away from God and closer to their own twisted ideas of who they are without God.

You may think pride is not one of your issues, but trust me, we all are full of pride. Even if you are a humble person, everyone has times in their lives where pride has raised its ugly head.

A great way to discover the pride issues in your life is to ask a trusted friend. You may have a blind spot where someone who knows you well can point out where he or she sees prideful actions in your life. This is tough to do, but finding areas of life that are choking out hearing God's voice is worth the embarrassment. Believe me, I have been there and as painful as it is to hear from my loved ones that I am bossy, pushy, and trying to plan their life is worth it to uncover areas that hinder my ability to hear God.

Thinking, *I can't do anything, I'm quiet, and people don't notice me* doesn't mean you don't have pride issues. Passive personalities are full of pride. They thrive on thinking of themselves by telling others that their thoughts don't matter; woe is me, poor me. Yuck! Pride in its most hidden form. It's time to open up with the truth and admit your prideful thoughts.

Let's go back and count the different issues in each list: Selfishness, Rebellion/Disobedience, Unforgiveness, and Pride. How many do you have? Maybe 100 or 50 different attitudes you've surrendered to God? I highly recommend you destroy each list into tiny pieces and burn them or toss them in the garbage where they belong. These are no longer who you are. You are forgiven, a child of God, friend of Christ, holy, a temple of the Holy Spirit, and much more. Celebrate! You are free from enormous blocks between you and hearing God's voice!

Taking these exercises seriously ensures that your mind is ready to experience the *10 Practical Experiments* as we move forward into the next chapters. Unforgiveness, Pride, Selfishness, Disobedience/Rebellion are no longer a part of who you are. So, who are you?

THREE

Who Am I?

THIS IS a question every person asks themselves in life.

We all wonder…

Why are we here on earth?

Why am I in this family?

What is the plan for my life?

These are significant questions with brilliant answers because it hinges on one essential thing:

Who are you?

Have you ever felt like everything you do turns out wrong? Or do you have a voice inside who nags you, saying you are stupid, no good, worthless, afraid of what will happen next, no one wants you or believes you?

It is essential that you know who you are because of what Jesus did for you. It's not on your own strength.

Once you understand who you are in Christ, life turns from a challenge to an opportunity—from fear and anxiety to boldness and confidence.

LET'S LOOK AT WHO GOD SAYS YOU ARE:

> "To all who received Him, who believed in His name, He gave the right to become children of God" (**John 1:12**).

> "Therefore, since we have been justified [just as if I never sinned] by faith, we have peace with God through our Lord Jesus Christ" (**Romans 5:1**).

> "Our citizenship is in Heaven, we wait for our Savior Jesus Christ" (**Philippians 3:20**).

> "Do you not know that you are God's temple and that God's Spirit lives in you" (**I Corinthians 3:16**)?

> "For we are His workmanship, created in Christ Jesus for good works, which God prepared ahead of time that we should walk in them" (**Ephesians 2:10**).

> "You are the salt of the earth and the light of the world" (**Matthew 5:13-14**).

> "I am Christ's friend" (**John 15:15**).

> "I have been bought with a price. I belong to God" (**1 Corinthians 6:20**).

LET'S GET STARTED

You need a pen, colored pencils/markers, and construction paper or copy paper.

First, ask God who you are because of what He has done. Then read each Scripture a few times. Think about what they are saying to you personally.

Next, take out your journal and write who God says you are from these passages, along with other Scriptures you know.

Finally, make a "Because I am" poster. Title the page "Because I am" and then write out all the true statements about yourself or the names God calls you. If something negative comes to mind get rid of it by speaking truth statements from His Word. You can make this as fun or simple as you like.

Now, hang it somewhere you can see as a daily reminder.

My website www.ConiKnepper.com includes other helpful statement pages you can make copies of or feel free to type up your own. Hang them somewhere in your home. Why? Because these are lifetime statements to remind you of the authority you have over negative thoughts in your mind. Anytime you say the name of Jesus, all demonic powers in your home have to flee. They no longer have any rights. You just ripped power from the enemy and opened up the floodgates for the Holy Spirit to overflow in you with love, boldness, compassion, confidence, and all the fruit of HIS SPIRIT.

EXAMPLE OF WHO I AM

In 1956, a premature baby was born into a world of witchcraft, abuse, fears, and a childhood of lies. She had a tiny, frail body and was unwanted by her parents, but loved by Jesus. Adults came and left with no explanation. As a child, thoughts occupied her mind. *I am no good, no one loves me, and I should be dead.*

In her teen years, suicide and sexual abuse ruled her until a group of people introduced her to Jesus. She surrendered her life to Him after hearing the Good News of how He loves her and died for all sins.

If you haven't already guessed, the little girl is me. My salvation as a teen is true; my freedom from doubt and confusion came much later, after I understood how to hear the voice of God.

Even after I turned over my life to Jesus, negative thoughts were confusing for me as an adult. I was a pastor's wife, a mother, and a Bible study leader. Why couldn't I control these thoughts? Because I didn't realize the power inside me. I had never learned how to hear God's voice. I didn't understand all of the voices competing for my attention were trying to destroy my life. To simply say that the name of Jesus gets rid of destructive thoughts is not a common teaching in the Church or anywhere. Neither is learning how to control the enemy's plans or replace destructive thoughts with God's words.

Sheesh, there are even Christ-followers who have a tough time believing there is a Satan or that he has influence when we sin.

It doesn't matter what the world portrays as truth or how other people view you, the crucial question is: Do you know Jesus? Do you listen to His voice and obey? When trouble comes, Jesus is the One who will never leave you nor turn His back on you. He LOVES YOU no matter what.

Freedom In Christ Ministries is a Christian organization with wonderful teachings. After years of study and training, I learned we are free from the past and free from generational sins. Sins passed down from your parents, grandparents—even four generations of sins can mess with your mind. Mine sure did.

I grew up with all these horrific sins done to me and around me. Yes, I had prayed the prayer of repentance and cried out to God to forgive me. I declared my alliance to Jesus as Lord, but nagging sins haunted me to live as if my life had not changed. My thoughts were full of fear and death. The voices still had control of my mind. Believing in Jesus saves you, however, filling your mind with His Word and obeying it is a game-changer. Taking control of the enemy by taking every thought captive keeps your mind free from fear, anxiety, suicidal thoughts, anger, and the list goes on. In the next few chapters, you will experience how to hear God's voice by participating in several activities. Satan doesn't want you to know he has a voice, and it is death.

Why do you think it is tough to pick up your Bible and read it? Because the enemy is tempting you to stray from God's Word. Satan desires anything else but listening to what God says. Why do you think your family has more fights on Sundays? Because the enemy doesn't want you to worship together or love each other. Satan plans to divide and devour with evil. You need to understand the battle is not against flesh and blood; the battle is for your mind, thoughts, and family.

> "For our struggle is not against flesh and blood, but against
> the rulers, against the authorities, against the powers of
> this dark world and against the spiritual forces of evil in
> the heavenly realms." —Ephesians 6:12

You see, God knew we would need to know this and be ready.

Even while writing this book, I had several attacks on my health and thought-life. But I know it's the enemy and I have confidence in how to stop his plans. These plans can help you get rid of any evil forces in your mind, home, school, or work place.

FOUR ESSENTIAL STEPS TO STOP THE ENEMY

#1 Worship

Sing and play worship songs in your home—every time the song gives glory to God or belts out the name of Jesus, the enemy has to flee. He has no strength to stay.

#2 Claim Jesus as Lord

More than saying you are a Christian—are you a Christ-follower? Do you look and operate differently? Do you forgive the people in your life from the previous chapter? Have you eliminated the pride, rebellion, and acts of selfishness? Remember, ignoring these things and pretending everything is okay does not make the enemy go away. It fuels his fire to cause confusion and internal struggles in your mind and heart.

Practice saying the "Because I am" statements out loud.

#3 Read the Word

Memorize it so you can quote it later when an anxious time occurs. Maybe you have nightmares and wake up frightened. You're not certain why worry is overwhelming your thoughts when something seems off. Start speaking out the truths of God's Word. Watch the dreams turn into a peaceful sleep. If that doesn't bring a night's rest, then maybe there is something you need to confess to God. Or, God woke you up to pray for someone else.

#4 Pray About Everything

Not "Grant me a safe life," but "Give me the courage to live this life you have gifted me." Not "Be with me Jesus," He is already *with* you. Ask Him to prepare you by bringing awareness of His ever-presence in your life.

Not "I want this or that," but "Lord, let Your will be done in my life and the life of others around me. Whatever it takes for _____ to surrender his/her life to Jesus as Lord and Savior."

EXAMPLE

My brother spent time in Folsom Prison and later died of brain cancer, but through it all, he turned over his life to Jesus and lived his last year with an enormous amount of love for God. He was a changed man, but it took hardships. I know I will see him again. Even on his dying bed, he praised God for his brain tumor because he knew if God had not allowed it, he may not have listened to the voice of his Heavenly Father and followed Him right into Jesus's arms in Heaven.

Prayers are powerful. I prayed for my brother faithfully for forty-three years and my mom, younger brother, and grandfather for twenty years. They all came to Jesus in dynamic ways, with the promise that we will see each other again in Heaven with new bodies, no further sickness, no more pain.

> "He will wipe every tear from their eyes. There will be no
> more death or mourning or crying or pain, for the old
> order of things has passed away." —Revelation 21:4

Sometimes we pray, "Whatever it takes, Lord," to join God in whatever life circumstance He might use to draw someone to Him. This doesn't, however, mean that whenever we pray this way, horrible sickness will occur. I don't believe God caused my family's illnesses, but He allowed them to alter our attention and trust Him. God works through whatever circumstances we encounter for what is best for every person. Our part is to pray and then trust God, especially when we are praying for someone's salvation.

Included in chapter 17 is a page of prayers for bedtime, morning prayer, prayers for freedom from fearful thoughts, along with lists of topical prayers I have prayed over the years. Praying is listening to God's voice and sharing your heart with Jesus.

FOUR

What's A Practical Experiment?

PRACTICAL EXPERIMENTS? What is that?

First, what it's not. You will not be using glass beakers or chemicals in these experiments. You won't need goggles to protect your face, but you will need something else to protect you, and that is your Bible. If you do not have one, Scriptures are provided inside each chapter.

The chapters also include a daily activity with a simple list of supplies required to prepare ahead of time. You will find everything you need from your home, again this is no "Mad Scientist."

After you try each Practical Experiment, continue back over your favorites and add them into the morning routine. When you begin your day with an experiment and in God's Word, your mind starts out refreshed and ready for whatever happens.

Chapters 5-14 instruct on how to hear God step-by-step and apply what you hear to your life every day. Experiencing listening to God is exciting, simple, and the best part of the day.

MORE DETAILS, PLEASE.

Glad you asked. It's a specific daily routine where you listen to God while actively engaging in a hands-on activity. The activities use your imagination while sharpening all five senses in hearing God. People hear God differently, which is why there are ten different spiritual experiments.

Several days involve manipulating unique elements like chalk or clay, which covers the touch senses. You are never too old to play.

Other experiments use your sight and hearing senses by noticing and listening through nature.

No, I don't mean trees are going to talk to you.

A few activities include short writings. These are important for further times with God while practicing your creative skills.

Scattered within each chapter are self-awareness questions to ensure you are on track with each experiment's purpose. These are for tracking your progress. Have fun! God is fun! Yes, He is all-powerful, all-knowing, but He is also loving, kind, and desires to be with you.

These Practical Experiments set you up to have an incredible time with Jesus.

Moving around or sitting still is your choice. As I shared earlier, my husband likes to sit still during his listening to God in the morning, while I like to dance around and MOVE. Both are correct because there is no right or wrong way, unless you choose to not take part in an experiment. Skipping an experiment means you miss out on what God has for you, but I believe if you have read this far, you are ready to tackle hearing God's voice for yourself.

It is crucial to develop a routine in hearing God daily. Time with God during the day is also necessary in equipping your heart to hear God's voice. We discussed it somewhat in the introduction, but I want to establish an under-standing.

First, you need to believe in Jesus Christ, surrender this time to Him and trust He will speak to you. To ease your mind and spirit, be ready, pray at the beginning of each Practical Experiment time.

Be honest with yourself and God about what is troubling you. Maybe you need to confess a sin or forgive someone. Let nothing block this time with you and Him.

It is strategic to plan the night before by collecting the supplies for the next day's experiment; it helps to not waste time, as I'm certain you are busy with other responsibilities. If you prepare ahead of time, it also ensures you will follow through the next morning.

I find it interesting that we plan for work, vacations, parties, etc., but for time with God, I often hear: "I just don't have time." Maybe because time with God has not been exciting? Ask yourself: How do you feel when your best friend or spouse longs to share an important event with you? You drop what you are doing to *be* with them. Correct?

The Maker of the universe wants to speak to *you*. He wants to be near you and share comforting, peaceful, and loving thoughts. The Holy Spirit is ready to lead you into an extraordinary life instead of a problematic dull existence. A life with a significant purpose.

Testimonies

Hands-on Practical Experiments may sound unusual, but trust me, my husband and I have been teaching these for years. Devin's testimony is one example of learning to listen to God's voice in practical ways and how it impacted his life and the life of his children.

Devin Alison—Santa Cruz, CA. Woodworker and Cabinet-maker

> One specific experience I remember trying was an experiment in learning to see what God may teach through the surrounding nature. After walking through sticks and over rocks in the woods, I found a place to sit on an old fallen log and asked God to show me what He might have for me next. I noticed a lizard on a boulder in front of me and asked God to speak through the experience. I watched and expected God to show me something. As the lizard just stayed in that spot doing what looked like push-ups as they do, I grew less patient wanting an answer, and that lizard would not move. I

threw something to scare it out of impatience. I'd wrecked the very thing I was asking for God to speak through. Then I heard that gentle voice of God speaking to my heart. *Be patient and wait.* It was a lesson in patience. I'll never forget. I still smile whenever I see a lizard and remember that lesson on waiting.

Another morning with Devin

> One morning, I was on the edge of a lake where I had gone to hear what God would speak to me. I was battling in my mind whether they should baptize me. I had known God from a young age, and everyone around me knew my devotion to Christ. So, why should I get baptized? I sat on the lakeside where I could see the fish below me. I'd searched my Bible, and now it was time to listen. What lesson would God have for me while watching the fish as the mist rises off the lake? *Those fish must be hungry*, I thought. There were plenty of bugs and all right in front of them. Why won't they eat? It's right in front of them. Until I realized what God had right in front of me. You will grow if you take what is in front of you. It was a lesson in obedience. I was baptized in that lake and grew to see more and more of who God has created me to be.

Spiritual Experiment Journal/Notebook

During every experiment, your time includes jotting down things God is whispering to you. For writing specific experiments, there are instructions on when to write in your journal/notebook as you go along.

It's time! Your mind is clear and you are ready to start the first experiment!

FIVE

Take a WIF- Who's It From?

PRACTICAL EXPERIMENT 1

YOU NEED PAPER, your journal, dark wide markers and your Bible.

PRACTICAL EXPERIMENT #1

When you whiff or breath you take in air. Take a full breath through your nose. Let it out through your mouth. God designed us to breathe. He's the One providing the air in your lungs. He also created your mind to understand what is true, lovely, pure, honorable, right, excellent, and praiseworthy. Remember your "Think About What You Think About" poster in Chapter 17?

Imagine a massive plate of your favorite food. It looks appetizing. The smell wafts past and you inhale deeply, anticipating your first bite. Hmm, it makes my mouth water thinking about a slice of pizza; it's a food not available where we live. I imagine putting the gooey cheesy pizza into my mouth.

It looks fantastic, smells fresh, and the mixture of bubbling cheese oozing over the side of the pan is tempting. You eat this same pizza from this shop frequently and have never become sick, so it must be okay to eat, correct?

We smell food before eating, inspecting what it looks like before trusting it enough to shovel it into our mouth. But if you've eaten it before, it's familiar and probably trustworthy. You know where it came from.

The same is true for your mind. You need to take a *WIF*. Ask yourself ***Who's It From***? Check it out, smell it, and see if you want to be thinking about it or sharing it with someone else. Your fears and worries cause other people to sin. Does the idea smell foul, sound not entirely true, or even represent a lie? The lies that have enough truth in them become easy to tuck into our thoughts without taking a WIF. Does the idea make you feel ashamed about yourself or others? Have you been here before? If so, it's from your self-talk, Satan, and his workers. He can't take away your salvation, but he can make you feel terrible about yourself, causing you the inability to follow through with the amazing things God has for you.

EXAMPLE

#1 A Daily WIF

Daily, I have to ask myself, *Are you thinking about the past and worrying about your children?* The second my thoughts go to the past, I stop and take a WIF. Who's it from? My self-talk, the enemy, my peers, or God? Are these thoughts wasting time in my day and causing undue worry and stress, which leads to sin and an open door for Satan to muddle my thoughts? Have I been down this road with these thoughts before? Did they lead to depression and guilt or encouraging actions? After doing this, I can stop quickly and not allow my thoughts to worsen. It takes practice taking a WIF; however, it is an excellent way to stay free.

#2 WHERE'S the Smell Coming From?

Where is the thought coming from? Take a WIF. Does it smell like trouble? "It's okay, my spouse, teacher, or friend will never know," but believe me, they always find out.

Is it a thought from your past that caused you to feel awful about yourself? Take a WIF. Ask yourself, whose thoughts are these? You, the enemy, God, peers? Is it a continuous habit? Ask God to help you. Begin filling your mind with His Word.

Are the thoughts from the enemy? You know he only wants to kill and destroy you through your thoughts, but you have the power to tell him *YOU* are the boss of your mind!

If it's from a peer, take a WIF. Are they trying to control you and guide you into trouble? Perhaps part of what they are saying is correct, but is it 100% true? You are the leader in your group of friends/family, leading them to conclusions that bring joy, peace, kindness, and a connection with Jesus. Not all friends understand their own thoughts and where they grow from. God will use you to encourage others in understanding how to connect with Jesus and hear His voice.

#3 DOWNLOADING THOUGHTS

Over twenty years ago, Jonathan Coates, a youth pastor in Washington attended our teachings on downloading your thoughts. After interviewing him, here's what he shared with me.

> Still, to this day, I download my thoughts so I can sleep at night. I have taught the kids in our children's ministry and youth ministry how to decide which thoughts are from God, from their self-talk, and from the enemy putting lies into their heads. I no longer feel like my thoughts at night are driving me crazy with worry.

The next section includes space to practice downloading your thoughts.

LET'S GET STARTED

First: Ask God to get rid of every thought in your head that is causing you anxiety, fear, or anything creating stress.

Next: Get out a piece of paper separate from your journal. For 60 seconds write every thought that comes into your mind. I call this downloading. It can be helpful when you can't sleep or turn off your thoughts. Download them. Write them down on paper as quickly as possible, whatever thought comes. It might be, "I wish I had a hot chocolate chip cookie." We don't have bakeries or chocolate chips. I crave cookies. I write that down. Usually it's more serious things that you need to stop thinking about.

Whatever the thoughts, write them down. God is guiding you because you asked Him to rid yourself of all stress.

Now: Look at what you wrote and inhale a WIF. Who's it from? Can you see anything from the enemy? Ask Jesus to kick these negative thoughts out of your mind and call out the name of Jesus. Speak out who you are, then cross them off the list. Using a heavy dark marker feels wonderful.

Take another WIF. Are there thoughts from yourself? Ongoing worries or fears? Ask God to comfort you and replace them with peace, joy, and sweet dreams. Confess to Jesus and make the decision to trust Him to take care of these matters. Write the words from Jesus over the worrisome self-talk. Again, a bold colored marker works well for this exercise.

Did you know worry is a sin? Worry often leads us to try to control a person or situation. We sin when we take control and choose to not depend on God. This leads to open doors for the enemy to gain control of our thoughts, which leads to confusion, doubt, and misery. You might find yourself asking, *Why do I feel lousy when nothing is wrong?* The problem is that *worry* is a *sin*! Confess the sin of worry to God and then move on; no sin is so great that God can not forgive you.

> "If we confess our sins, He is faithful and just and will forgive
>   us our sins and purify us from all unrighteousness."
> —1 John 1:9

Thoughts from God, however, bring comfort, instruction, and encouragement. Write them in your journal. If you don't hear thoughts from God to download, ask Him to speak to you. Wait, and He will. Write it down in your journal.

Lastly, take the paper with *your* thoughts and tear it up into tiny pieces, toss it into the trash, or burn it in the fireplace.

These thoughts no longer belong in your mind. You took control of the enemy; you are the boss of your mind. You hugely connected with Jesus. It may not feel like it, but you are *free* from negative conversations in your mind causing anxiety, worry, fear, stress, and a list of other things God did not plan for you to think about. This takes practice, just as all the practical experiments do, but they are spiritually life-changing if you try them. The enemy and your own thoughts will try and dive back into your mind. Freedom takes practice. Don't give up, that is exactly what the deceiver wants you to do.

SIX

Now What?

WE'VE COVERED a lot of ground in these initial five chapters. How are you holding up?

Are you hanging in there with me? Are you able to take a WIF and recognize what voices are clambering for your attention?

I promise the next chapters involve you and God having time together.

If you feel overwhelmed and unsure, these Practical Experiments are for you. Joy for Jesus will ooze out of your pores for more Jesus-connections after experiencing hearing God's voice.

Make sure you have completed the previous check-off lists. Then take time to meditate on who you are because of what Jesus Christ accomplished on the cross.

A new journal is a good idea when preparing for a unique experience.

Prepare when and where you will set out your experiments. I understand a ten-day commitment is significant, but you are not doing this to finish a book and stack it on the rest of your past adventures in reading. This one is unique; it's designed especially for you and Jesus to connect, maybe for the first time. By completing these experiments, you are entering a period of life in which you can look forward to saying, "Wow, I can hear the voice of God and know the difference between His voice, my own, the enemy, and peers in my life. Jesus loves me, and I know it from experience."

Of course, none of this is possible unless you put in some effort. Prepare, pray, and expect to hear from God—and you will.

If you feel confused, remember confusion is not from Jesus; it is from the enemy. Take a WIF and then kick out negative thoughts by proclaiming the name of Jesus. He is your power source.

I wrote this book for you to experience freedom in knowing Christ personally—for freedom from fears, anxiety, and doubts about who you are. Be free to hear God and all He has to share with you.

I care about your mind and know my prayer team is praying for you.

Email me with questions. I would *love* to hear your testimonies:

coniknepper@gmail.com

Now, have fun with Jesus!

SEVEN

Nature and the Great Outdoors

PRACTICAL EXPERIMENT 2

CHOOSE A DAY WITH GOOD WEATHER, your journal, and something to write with.

PRACTICAL EXPERIMENT #2

NATURE- (NOTICING *God*)

Notice nature, or better yet, *go* outside.

Ask God to show Himself to you in nature.

What do you notice?

What reminds you of God's love for you?

How can you praise God today?

Journal what God shows you, or sketch a picture of nature.

These are some of the questions that make up your Nature Experiment.

. . .

THIS PRACTICAL EXPERIMENT includes your journal and something to write with: old school fun, no computers. Remember to pray first, a simple prayer asking God to speak to you today. Let Him know if you need to tell Him a hurt in your heart, a lie you might have told, or any sin you are struggling with. *Be honest* —express everything before you start. Then ask Him to make your heart pure.

> "Wash away all my wickedness and cleanse me from my sin."
> —Psalms 51:2

> "You will seek me and find me when you seek me with all your heart." —Jeremiah 29:13

> "Create in me a clean heart, O God, and renew a right spirit within me." —Psalms 51:10

Ready? Let's get started on an outdoor adventure.

Outside reflects the character of God. He is the perfect author of all that is good.

What did He say in Genesis while He created?

This is good. In Genesis 1:21,

> "God created the great creatures of the sea and every living thing with which the water teems and that moves about in it, according to their kinds, and every winged bird according to its kind. And God saw that it was GOOD."

> "Everything God created is good, and nothing is to be rejected if it is received with thanksgiving." —1 Timothy 4:4

We won't be listening for rocks to cry out or trees to worship God, but we *will* notice creation.

If weather permits, take a brief trip outside or look out a window. What do you notice?

At first, it may seem like things you've seen a million times. Trees, grass, cement walkways, apartments, or homes lined up in an orderly fashion. But what if you look closer and listen?

Start writing everything, even the obvious: your yard, home, trees, etc.

Next, get on your hands and knees and look inside the grass or between the cement cracks. Don't mind the neighbors; they already know you are slightly strange. What do you see?

If you can only look out a window, look farther away than your yard. Look up towards the sky; what do the clouds look like? Any mountains? Any lakes or rivers you can glimpse in the distance? Write everything that you can see (Proverbs 24:30-34).

Observation is key in this experiment: What is God revealing to you in how the bugs scurry in circles?

EXAMPLE OF NATURE JOURNAL ENTRIES.

I noticed a group of bugs running through the grass, seeming very busy but going where? As I watched, God reminded me that I need to slow down and take a break, to rest. The bugs ran in and out of the dirt; they had a purpose, and I have a purpose, but I frequently try to do many tasks at once. God revealed to me how I lack focus by trying to do many seemingly important things in a single day. I can become prideful in my multitasking and then burn out with exhaustion. All this just from noticing and observing a group of bugs in the yard.

Laugh with Jesus at the shapes of the clouds or the configuration of a tree. Enjoy your time listening, learning, and sharing what you see with Jesus, your friend.

Life lessons are everywhere. Ask God to remove the confusion in your mind and replace it with more of Him.

Examining nature can cause you to praise and thank God for a specific situation in your life or confront you on an issue you need to work on. Nonetheless, every nature walk is different for every person. One thing is true: if you ask God, He will show you Himself.

Here is where it gets creative and fun!

Take your paper and draw whatever you like as you listen to God, revealing to you something about nature and creation. Some people draw doodles with different shades and shapes. I have seen some beautiful pictures, surrounded by words of praise to God.

Like all the experiments, there is no wrong way to listen to God. Your paper design is about how you observe creation and then praise God for it. Try to record some kind of title across the top of your paper. Write a comment or two describing how you feel, a verse, a saying, anything that will benefit you in remembering the time you and Jesus explored outside and noticed God. How powerful He is, how loving He is, or how creative He is. He lives in you, which means you also can possess these attributes. When you are loving, kind, creative, powerful, able to listen, those come from the Holy Spirit living in you. How does that make you feel? To know Jesus's very Spirit lives in you and wants to lead you into the presence of God so you can hear Him speak to you is incredible.

WOW! Our God is awesome!

Next, write a brief description in your journal. Every day requires an entry. It can be a few words or complete sentences. Write something that reminds you of what you and Jesus experienced together.

EXAMPLE

My journal entry from the day I saw the bugs:

> *"Jesus, thank You for showing me how busy I get running in circles when You have a bigger purpose for my life. I ask for forgiveness for being prideful. Today, I choose to repent of pride and ask You to fill me with humility and love for others first.*
>
> *1/19/2020"*

Remember to date all your entries. TADA! That's it.

Later, I wrote a more extended conversation as Jesus kept showing me more about those bugs. It doesn't have to be a big deal with pressure to write some fantastic story. If you have one, great, but if you just want to say, "Thank You," that's enough. It's your thoughts with your time, not anyone else's.

EIGHT

Love Letter A

PRACTICAL EXPERIMENT 3

YOU NEED paper of various shades, glue, scissors, your journal, markers, and something to write with.

PRACTICAL EXPERIMENT #3

Writing a letter can seem intimidating or a waste of time, but what if the letter is for someone who loves you more than anyone else can?

God wrote 66 books to you within the Bible. They are letters to churches, groups of people, and *you*. God loves you more than you can imagine, but wait, let's try to imagine through creating a letter. I told you that I will not say He loves you without offering a way to experience that love.

Do you hear nagging voices in your head that no one loves you or that your sins are so great, God will never love you? Do you feel like God's love is far off and for someone else?

Get those lies out of your head! Lies come from the enemy as explained in chapter 3. Take those tormenting thoughts and tell them where to go, out of your head!

Then, ask God to replace them with more faith, strength, joy, and peace. Ask out loud in the name of Jesus and keep it up until the lies leave your thoughts. You may not feel any different, but the enemy knows he has been defeated by the power of Jesus's name. Move on leaving negative thoughts behind you.

Why do I need to speak things out loud? Simply because the enemy can not hear what you are thinking. He can not be in your mind—he can tempt you with generic thoughts of doubt, fear, and shame, but he does not know you personally like Jesus does. Which means if you are telling a thought to get out of your head and you are saying it mentally in your mind, then the enemy doesn't hear. Speaking out loud gives you authority because you hear it which affects your self-talk in a positive way. Trust me, speak those inner struggles out loud and tell them in the name of Jesus to leave your mind and you will see results.

My guess is that it's been forever since you've hand written a love letter. That's okay, but for this Practical Experiment you need paper and a pen or pencil, no keyboards, please. Normally, typing is fine, but for this experiment you only need a piece of paper and something to write with.

The letter you are about to compose is for God Almighty, the maker of all things, all-powerful and all-knowing, He is everywhere at all times, and He longs to hear from you. Take a moment to reflect on the immeasurable things God has done. Think about the attributes of God; who is He? Even though He knows you better than anyone else, He still wants to hear from your heart.

GOD IS

1. God is infinite.

> *"And He is before all things, and in Him all things hold together."* —
> *Colossians 1:17*

You are safe with God.

· · ·

2. God never changes.

> *"I the Lord do not change. So you, the descendants of Jacob, are not destroyed."* —Malachi 3:6

You can trust God.

3. God is all powerful.

> *"By the word of the Lord the heavens were made, their* starry *host by* the breath *of His mouth."* —Psalm 33:6

God protects you.

4. God is all-knowing.

> *"You see, at just the right time, when we were still powerless, Christ died for the ungodly. 7Very rarely will anyone die for a righteous person, though for a good person someone might possibly dare to die. But God demonstrates his own love for us in this: While we were still sinners, Christ died for us."* —Romans 5:6-8

God knows you and still loves you.

5. God is always everywhere.

> "Where can I go from your Spirit? Or where can I flee from Your presence? If I go up to the heavens, You are there; If I make my bed in the depths, You are there. If I rise on the wings of the dawn, if I settle on the far side of the sea, even there Your hand will guide me, And Your right hand will hold me fast." —Psalm 139:7-10

You are never alone.

6. God is good.

> "O, taste and see that the Lord is good. Evil happens, but
> none of those who take refuge in Him will be condemned."
> —Psalm 34

God is inviting you to experience His goodness.

LOVE LETTERS DON'T HAVE to be gushy with xoxoxo—they can be, but if you communicate better without hearts and roses, no worries. God knows; He created you.

LET'S START.

First, ask God to clean out your mind and heart so you can hear Him. Make certain you're not holding anything against anyone. Confess unforgiveness, then talk to God about the issue.

> "Then I acknowledged my sin to you and did not cover up my
> iniquity. I said, 'I will confess my transgressions to the
> Lord,' and you forgave the guilt of my sin." —Psalm 32:5

Next, close your eyes and imagine God as the Holy Spirit sitting right next to you. What do you want to say to Him?

Last, write what you are going through to God. Some "feelings" are hard to articulate, and that's okay. Write whatever comes to mind. Try drawing a picture or write a few statements of thankfulness to God.

This exercise is for you and God to connect, there is no wrong way to express your love. The objective is to take time during your day to acknowledge how much He means to you through a love letter.

I enjoy expressing to God how I love and appreciate Him by listing the things I appreciate about my children, grandchildren, our ministry in Africa, and my salvation.

Love letters call out for decorations. For the artists in the group, create a border around your letter or add a design. Writing your letter on stationary can help bring out the creative side. Imagine writing a letter to the love of your life or your best friend—you desperately long for them to know how you care. How would the letter look? This letter is for Jesus. He is your advocate and promises never to hurt you, leave you, lie to you, or stop loving you; He can't stop caring about you.

> "In the same way, the Spirit helps us in our weakness. We do
> not know what we ought to pray for, but the Spirit himself
> intercedes for us through wordless groans."
> —Romans 8:26

Jesus would not be Jesus if held grudges or stopped loving you.

You might be tempted to think, *This is juvenile or silly, I'm a grown person, not a child creating a card for someone.*

But are you? God says we are His child and that children will see God. Think about it. Have you grown into an adult that has forgotten how to be with God?

After you complete your love letter with all the bells and whistles, or simply written on white typing paper, tuck it into your journal to refer to it in Love Letter B in the next chapter.

NINE

Love Letter B
PRACTICAL EXPERIMENT 4

YOU NEED paper of various colors or stationary, markers, and something to write with.

PRACTICAL EXPERIMENT #4

For some of you, writing a letter to Jesus came easy. For others, it might have been a challenge; don't give up. I'm switching it up, meaning this Practical Experiment will be the opposite of what you wrote last time. You are writing a letter *from* Jesus to *you*.

After completing at least three experiments, I promise this one will blow your mind. Why? Because this is a time to sit and listen to God, no objects to move, no pictures to draw, or colors to blend, it's all you and Jesus.

Believe me, when you finish writing this letter, your heart will be full of amazement. How can I say that? Because for the last forty-five years of leading teens, children, and adults into the presence of God, this experiment is always a favorite. It doesn't matter your gender or age, hearing God and writing in letter form will transform your heart and mind if you take it seriously. God wants to talk with you. LISTEN.

• • •

LET'S GET STARTED.

First, you need to invite the Holy Spirit to make you aware of His presence. People pray to ask the Holy Spirit to be with them or, *please don't leave me.* That makes no sense. There is no need to worry about the Holy Spirit leaving you; His presence is never-ending. The Holy Spirit does not jump in and out of your soul. Since the Holy Spirit lives in you forever, that means He wants to speak to you. Remember the treasures we talked about earlier, how God wants to share His amazing knowledge with you? He has words and thoughts for only you to hear from Himself. WOW! How does that make you feel? Review other experiments you have completed and reread how Jesus specifically spoke to you.

Next, you need to have your journal ready, a favorite paper much like you did for Love Letter A, and your Bible. When God speaks, many times, it is through His Word, which we will discuss more in Chapter 11.

Finally, *"be still and know that I am God"* (Psalm 46:10).

Allow God to speak to your mind and heart. Start your letter with: "Dear (your name)." Ask God: "What do You want to tell me today?"

Ideas and phrases will come to mind; write them down. Pause and then ask, *God, I need to hear from You. What do You think about me?*

As thoughts come, add them to your letter from God. Keep writing until you feel a peaceful end. Then, end your letter with: "I love you, from Jesus."

A KEEPSAKE

After you finish writing your letter from Jesus to you, keep it where you can see it and ponder on the words God spoke. Decorate your letter with pictures and borders, much like the other letter from you to God. I recommend writing a letter from God once a month. It is good to remind yourself how God feels about you. If you hear a verse, include it in your letter, then highlight and date it in your Bible.

EXAMPLE

Kylie is our oldest grandchild. She struggles with believing God has anything to say to her. The first time we did this experiment, she felt far from God. She sat waiting patiently and then said out loud, "This will not work for me." I gently prayed with her and explained how it takes time to know you are hearing God.

"How about if you ask Him for a verse in the Bible?" We prayed and asked God to show her a personal verse—something she could learn from. After a couple of minutes, an unfamiliar verse came to mind. We looked it up together and BOOM! It said something specific about what she was feeling. With tears in her eyes, she wrote out the love letter from Jesus.

The answer won't be quick or specific every time, but God knew Kylie needed encouragement. He knows what you need, but it takes believing, being still, and listening.

I have every letter God has spoken to me over the years. Looking back on the encouraging words eliminates doubts or confusion from my mind.

The next experiment involves more of a hands on approach to listening to God. I can't wait to show you how!

TEN

Chalk Talk

PRACTICAL EXPERIMENT 5

YOU NEED PAPER, different shades of chalk, and your journal.

PRACTICAL EXPERIMENT #5

In the Chalk Talk Experiment, using chalk to listen to God's voice does not require you to be an artist.

If you enjoy drawing and find it's a way to express yourself, then great, but an art project is not what "chalk conversations" are designed for. This needs to be clear, otherwise, you may give up before you start.

There is nothing holy about chalk; it's a medium to doodle your thoughts and express yourself to the Creator of chalk. People doodle all the time. I fill my office with pieces of scratch paper marbled with doodle markings. My friends and family know that if you leave an envelope or an important paper around, it will end up covered in squiggles. Imagine all the receipts and notes in your home with doodle marks on them. Well, that's me.

Your chalk talk can be a jumble of doodles connecting with intersections over the page. Or, it can be a mass of various colors overlapping one another using the side of your chalk. Chalk talks are as different as a sunset. Or, maybe yours *is* a sunset.

LET'S START.

First, pray and ask God to replace any bad thoughts or weariness with energy and images of kindness, joy, peace, and self-control. Forgive those people who might have upset you. Ask God to speak to you today while you are creating with chalk. You are ready to have fun with Jesus.

CREATE! Be in a quiet place where no one will watch you design — then create your chalk talk.

Ask God to reveal to you where you need an attitude or character transformation. Then, ask God to work in you to do just that — change.

Let your feelings out. If you are cheerful, show it on paper and tell Jesus you are excited about Him and what you two are doing together. If you are feeling depressed or serious, use your chalk to create with shapes and colors. Drag your chalk across the paper — what do you see? What do you feel? How is God whispering to you? Listen, He has a plan He wants to create with you. If a memory comes to mind, draw the experience. This is Jesus speaking to your heart. Remember, there is no wrong chalk talk.

EXAMPLE

My latest chalk talk consisted of the flat side of pastel colored chalks. I asked God for a word from Him. Just one word, and the word FAITH came to mind. I rubbed the chalk across my journal page back and forth overlapping the colors. Then I took a deep blue color and wrote the word FAITH with a pink cross in the background. The cross faded as if the word faith was holding it up. As I sat listening and meditating on the word faith the realization that I need to have faith to accomplish the ministries God is calling me to do in Tanzania came to the forefront. I need more faith and the only place it is coming from is the cross, JESUS. After several minutes of sitting still my heart revealed that I need to repent and ask Jesus for more faith. The picture is in my journal with a date and short explanation of the time Jesus and I spent together. It's simple—no amazing art work, but with a powerful message I needed that day.

JOURNAL TIME

Take a long look at your chalk talk." What is God showing you about Himself or yourself? Stand back and admire what you and Jesus created together. You can frame it as a showpiece or slide it into your journal.

Speaking of your journal, use it! Fill entries with swooshes and swipes of colors and lines. Detail your chalk time with specific definitions, then date the page in your journal.

When I have an extraordinary time with Jesus, I put a star next to the date in my journal to remind me each time I glance back at the amazing experience I had with Jesus.

Some of your experiments will call for an extra folder to display oversized experiments.

I encourage you to review these over the years. Memories of listening to God and kicking negative thoughts out of your head are times to appreciate, whether five minutes or an hour, whatever time you have, God honors it.

Side note, some people like using paints as their medium for this experiment. Paints work well if chalk is not something you prefer to use.

If you are skipping around the Practical Experiments, maybe doing them out of order, make sure you do not skip this one. Each chapter is designed to do on their own on separate days, however none of them are meant to be pushed aside, especially the next chapter.

ELEVEN

His Voice

PRACTICAL EXPERIMENT 6

You need your journal, Bible, and something to write with.

PRACTICAL EXPERIMENT #6

Have you ever heard God's audible voice? People don't think they have, but what about the Bible?

It is God's words.

> "All Scripture is God-breathed and is useful for teaching,
>   rebuking, correcting and training in righteousness."
> —*2 Timothy 3:16*

It says all Scripture is breathed by God; they complete you and equip you for good works.

Did you hear it? You just heard the words of God! His Spirit is *in* you, which means when you speak God's words you are being used by Him to share His voice. Isn't that exciting?! You can hear God's voice just by reading His word! God's people benefit by sharing what you read.

When was the last time you were mesmerized by the scriptures instead of the world? Or been overwhelmed to the point of tears after reading the wonders in God's message instead of being overwhelmed by all that is happening in today's news?

In these times, it's easy to spiral into dark thoughts. Discovering who God is through each experiment provides a way out of the darkness and into the light of Jesus. First Peter 2:9 says, "*We are called out of darkness into his marvelous light.*"

LET'S GET STARTED.

You need your journal, Bible, and something to write with. I have included verses for you to read, meditate, and pray on.

Meditation means to think about and ask God what He wants you to learn from the verses. There is nothing mystical about meditating. Joshua 1:8 says to *"meditate on the word day and night so that you may be careful to do according to all that is written in it."* Think about God's Word; let it permeate your mind with peace and replace doubt and fears. The enemy prowls around, drawing you away from Scripture. He wants you to be full of fear and confusion. An effective way to kick negative thoughts out of your head is to replace them with the truth of God's Word.

First, read the Bible verses several times from the *Bible page* provided. Slowly read over each verse, asking God to speak to you.

Next, while you are asking God to speak, notice if specific words jump out or point to meaningful verses to you. If you notice an emotion, pause and re-read those scriptures again.

Finally, write the verse or verses in your journal with the day's date.

The Big Question. What is God saying to you in these verses? Write in your journal what you discovered in your heart. It takes practice to hear God daily. Time spent developing ears that hear, beyond the noise of this world, means that less confusion and doubt will play a part in your thinking.

In the beginning of practicing hearing God through Scripture, a couple of words of encouragement may be all you hear, however, be patient. In no time, you will find God giving you verses speaking to the issues you are dealing with.

If you feel stuck, don't give up trying; that is precisely what your self-talk and the enemy hope for. Keep asking for God's guidance and then read the verses several times, over and over. Sometimes moving onto another section of verses helps.

I have read verses and thought, *Why do I need to know this?* Then, later in the day, I find those verses bring me comfort or help for someone else. I needed exactly the verses God showed me earlier in the day, which is another positive reason to do your Practical Experiments in the morning. Years ago, God brought the page numbers in my Bible to mind, and I found the verses spoke to me. However you hear God guide you, make sure to remember that it's *Him.* It's easy to think it's *our* own thoughts guiding us, which turns into pride. Yuck!

EXAMPLE

After praying and seeking God for the title of this book, I ran through many scenarios. It started out as *Is That You, God?* But it's overused; too many books with the same title.

Then the title changed to *Know Greater Joy.* A good friend shared what the words meant to her, which sounded great until I put it out to a group of readers and authors, all of whom said they wouldn't purchase that title. UGH! Remember, your believing friends are a tremendous help in making life decisions.

The night before I submitted my book to the editor for approval, I asked God *again,* "What do You want the title to be for our book?" My head was full of all kinds of frustration while trying to figure out a title on my own strength. In frustration, I spoke out loud, "Get Out Of My Head!"

YES!

Then God allowed me to feel His presence and know that this is the title He wants for this book. God reminded me why He called me to write *Get Out Of My Head*. He spoke these words to my heart.

I long to teach people how to hear His voice and be free from confusion, fear, doubts, and lies from the enemy. My dark life of death left me over thirty years ago to show others how to tune in to the voice of God and kick the darkness of confusion out of their minds.

Determine to listen to God's voice and get everything else out of your head by replacing it with the truth of Scripture.

The point is, I asked God to help me write this book and give me a title. It took a few tries to find the right one; God leads if we don't give up. I needed to go through the process with Him to know that *Get Out Of My Head: 10 Practical Ways to Replace Internal Struggles with Knowing the Voice of God* is what He wanted. The 10 Practical Ways ended up on the back of the cover, but it's there.

The Word of God also includes the power to change a person's heart and clear their mind. We talked about speaking out the name of Jesus, which is powerful enough to chase the enemy away. Imagine if you spoke out sections of God's Word. WOW! The truth will set you free.

If you read God's Word and obey it, then the truth of His Word will set YOU FREE!

> "If you hold to my teaching, you are really my disciples. hen
> you will know the truth, and the truth will set you free."
> —*John 8:31-32*

> "Love the Lord your God with all your heart, with all your
> soul, with all your mind, and with your strength."
> —Mark 12:30

Proof of His Word

Everyone looks at God's Word individually, however if you are a follower of Jesus then you have the Holy Spirit leading you, speaking to you to understand God's words.

Some believe it's out of date and there's no reason to read the Bible. I believe there is power in reading God's Word because the 66 books in the Bible are God's plan for His people: us.

It is the breath of God. He spoke through the authors of the Bible to point people to Jesus, our Savior. There are no contradictions, no lies, and all promises are, or will be, fulfilled. The Old Testament sets the stage for the New, while both speak of a Savior coming back to take us home. No other book has outlasted the truth of God's Word. When you read it, it changes your life forever.

How can I be so confident? Well, for a couple of reasons—God has never failed me when I read His word and He accomplishes what He says He will do and is who He says He is. Never has He changed and gone back on a promise. This doesn't mean God answers all prayers the way I want, but it means God always answers prayers.

In the next chapter I hope to stir up sweet childhood memories by using an old familiar manipulative.

VERSUS **for the Bible Practical Experiment**

> *"Search me, God, and know my heart, test me, and know my anxious thoughts. See if there is any offensive way in me, and lead me in the way everlasting." —Psalm 139:23-24*

This is a great prayer for yourself and others daily.

> "My soul is weary with sorrow; strengthen me according to your word." —Psalm 119:28

> "Give me understanding, so that I may keep your law and obey it with all my heart. Direct me in the path of your commands, for there I find delight." —Psalm 119:34-35

> "And pray in the Spirit on all occasions with all kinds of

prayers and requests. With this in mind, be alert and always keep on praying for all the Lord's people."
—Ephesians 6:18

"Trust in the Lord with all your heart and lean not on your own understanding; in all your ways submit to him, and he will make your paths straight." —Proverbs 3:5-6

"Take delight in the Lord, and he will give you the desires of your heart." —*Psalms 37:4*

I enjoy praying these scriptures for my husband:

"For this reason, since the day we heard about you, we have not stopped praying for you. We continually ask God to fill you with the knowledge of his will through all the wisdom and understanding that the Spirit gives, so that you may live a life worthy of the Lord and please him in every way: bearing fruit in every good work, growing in the knowledge of God, being strengthened with all power according to his glorious might so that you may have great endurance and patience, and giving joyful thanks to the Father, who has qualified you to share in the inheritance of his holy people in the kingdom of light. For he has rescued us from the dominion of darkness and brought us into the kingdom of the Son he loves, in whom we have redemption, the forgiveness of sins." —Colossians 1:9-14

"Teach me your way, Lord, that I may rely on your faithfulness, give me an undivided heart, that I may fear your name." —Psalm 86:11

Start the day praying one of these scriptures:

"The Lord has done it this very day; let us rejoice today and be glad." —Psalm 118:24

"Therefore, as God's chosen people, holy and dearly loved, clothe yourselves with compassion, kindness, humility, gentleness, and patience." —Colossians 3:12

(Clothe yourself on the inside before getting dressed on the outside.)

"He has shown you, O mortal, what is good. And what does the Lord require of you? To act justly and to love mercy and to walk humbly with your God." —Micah 6:8

"Create in me a pure heart, O God, and renew a steadfast spirit within me." —Psalm 51:10

"I remain confident of this: I will see the goodness of the Lord in the land of the living." —Psalm 27:13

"He said to them, "Go into all the world and preach the gospel to all creation." —Mark 16:15

"This, then, is how you should pray: 'Our Father in heaven, hallowed be your name, your kingdom come, your will be done, on earth as it is in heaven. Give us today our daily bread. And forgive us our debts, as we also have forgiven our debtors, and lead us not into temptation, but deliver us from the evil one.'" —Matthew 6:9-13

End the day praying one of these scriptures

"The Lord your God is with you, the Mighty Warrior who saves. He will take great delight in you; in his love he will no longer rebuke you, but will rejoice over you with singing." —Zephaniah 3:17

"Come to me, all you who are weary and burdened, and I will give you rest." —Matthew 11:28

"Therefore do not worry about tomorrow, for tomorrow will worry about itself. Each day has enough trouble of its own." —Matthew 6:34

"In vain you rise early and stay up late, toiling for food to eat —for he grants sleep to those he loves." —Psalm 127:2

"When you lie down, you will not be afraid; when you lie down, your sleep will be sweet." —Proverbs 3:24

"In peace I will lie down and sleep, for you alone, Lord, make me dwell in safety." —Psalm 4:8

"I lie down and sleep; I wake again, because the Lord sustains me." —Psalm 3:5

Once you start praying Scripture your heart longs for more. Write out some of your favorite Scriptures and see how you can transform them into prayers to Jesus Christ.

Then underline in your Bible the meaningful ones that touched your heart while praying.

Enjoy God's words to you—remember, He is speaking to YOU personally through His Word.

TWELVE

Claying Around

MOLD ME AND MAKE ME LIKE YOU JESUS - EXPERIMENT 7

YOU WILL NEED a small amount of color clay, your journal, a camera, and something to write with.

PRACTICAL EXPERIMENT #7

As a child, I loved it when my grandmother bought me soft clay. It came in six basic colors and smelled like nothing else. Its own odor made my heart jump, as I thought about the unusual way to roll it and mold it into different creatures and shapes. No matter what I did, squeezing it through my fingers brought me the most delight. It's funny how a lump of clay can bring about warm feelings.

> "But, now, Lord, you are our father. We are the clay, and you
> are our potter. We are the work of your hands."
> —Isaiah 64:8

Let's get started.

First, you need a small amount of your favorite color clay. It's perfectly fine to mix and match colors, whatever brings out the most imagination and creativity in you. Find a quiet place without distractions, somewhere you can be away from others in your home or outside. You may need to carve out time before everyone rises or after they retire to bed. Much like the previous experiments, it requires time to ask God to speak to you.

Next, share with God how you feel today. Is there something bothering you? Do you feel lonely or disappointed in someone or something? Is anger getting the best of your response to others? If so, explain to God everything. Then, seek Him to replace these feelings with the joy of knowing that He is with you and wishes to hear your voice.

Lastly, the fun begins. Take your clay and roll it, smash it, have fun for no particular reason. Touch and squeeze it through your fingers. Pretend you are in Kindergarten again. Ask God, "Why did you form me? Why do you think I am special?"

Create something as it comes to your mind. Ask God, "What do you think of me?" This is an excellent chance to seek God for what He wants to show you. Keep rolling and forming the clay into any shape or design that reveals what is running through your thoughts. If Scripture comes to mind, note it down. God loves to speak to people through His Word.

Afterward, enter what you created into your journal. Write how you felt and why your clay formed into the various shapes or designs.

This experiment won't fit in your journal, but you can take a picture and save it on your phone. Print it out later and hang it up somewhere in your home as a reminder of your time playing with Jesus using clay. Remembering times you discovered God's voice will stick better if you collect your pictures. It doesn't mean your "Clay Around" is always light-hearted. Here are some examples of meaningful times I experienced.

EXAMPLES

If you think these may influence how your clay experiment turns out, then don't read these. If you need help in understanding how "Clay Around" works, then read about others' experiences.

Listed below are clay experiments that have stayed with me over the years. Some are my own experiences and some are from students.

#1 A CLUMSY-LOOKING CLAY ANIMAL, **all alone, drinking at a fountain overflowing with clay spouts of water**

Alone and thirsty, it prompted me to feel my own thirst for companions. I was feeling like an outcast from my family and friends. I shared with God how often I missed them. Jesus caused a calming in my heart and mind. He reminded me that He is my best friend and will never give up on me. The verses about Jesus being springs of living water came to mind. I looked them up and jotted them down in my journal. It brought me comfort in a time of heartache.

#2 A THIN **road of clay laid out with offshoots of other roads leading to nowhere. At the end of the road, a wall stood, barring further travel. Beyond the wall lay a massive clay butterfly decorated in rows of matching dots and swirls, all in the same dark green color.**

The young lady explained how the roads led to various places, but she didn't know which one to travel. The wall closing off the road from finding the butterfly caused her sadness. I asked her what the wall meant. Her response went something like this, "I want to be on the road following God, but something keeps stopping me from hearing Him." She peeled the clay away from the plain green butterfly and underneath was a vivid colored beautiful butterfly. "This is who I long to be."

We discussed how life has many choices leading to places that might hurt you. The wall represented the enemy and her negative self-talk, which brought up all kinds of Scripture. The young woman is working on her journey with Jesus. It doesn't suddenly make everything fine. Immediate *gladness* isn't the point of the practical experiments. Each one is designed to help you hear God's voice and listen to what He's saying to you and then obey what you hear. If you plan on skipping the obeying step, you can count on repeating the same issues continuously.

. . .

#3 A HANDPRINT on a lump of clay formed into a half-moon shape. The opening resembled a clamshell. Inside the shell was a tiny ladder with a round gumdrop shape "walking" up the ladder into the shell.

While creating with this clay, I thought what I was working on were separate words from God. As I prayed, I realized the clamshell shape with the handprint was God's hands holding me, the little gumdrop. The ladder leading inside the clamshell was short, easy to walk right in. This reminded me of how simple and easy God makes salvation. It's not about me; I'm only a gumdrop in His large hands. He protects me, loves me, and surrounds my life with his hands.

#4 AN ENORMOUS mouth with an elongated tongue emerging out of the open hole. Next to the mouth lay a heart perfectly shaped, but broken on one end.

As I started my clay time with Jesus, I first felt nothing as I rolled clay into two balls. I asked God what He wanted of me today. The first ball became a smiling face with a large open mouth. Immediately, I thought of a tongue flapping between the smiles. The second ball of clay seemed to make a perfectly shaped heart. As I listened to God tug at my heart, something struck me. This smile is my mouth with a never-ending wagging tongue talking all the time. The broken heart represented God's heart. My mouth gets me in trouble regularly. Staring at the two shapes, it was clear I needed to confess my sinful talking about others. Breaking God's heart is never my intention, but God needed me to *see* what my mouth was doing.

As you can see, claying around can be insightful if you take the time to listen and obey. It is one of my favorite experiments, however in the next chapter you will be blown away when you see how God has a specific life message for you. All you have to do is ask.

THIRTEEN

Your Life Verse

PRACTICAL EXPERIMENT 8

YOU NEED YOUR JOURNAL, Bible, and something to write with.

PRACTICAL EXPERIMENT #8

You have been studying how to listen to God and hear His voice. You have practiced using many elements, encouraging you how to hear the voice of God.

Now, it's time to ask Him the big question. *What is my life verse?* All the Bible verses are for us, but God has one or a section that He chooses to show you.

EXAMPLE

My story takes place several years back, but it's a day etched in my memory forever.

In my junior year of high school I heard about Jesus for the first time. Holidays like Christmas meant gifts and Santa. Easter included running around hunting for brightly colored eggs in a $0.99 basket with strings of fake grass that seemed to stick to everything. No matter how much you clean it up, by summer you find Easter grass under a cushion or in the car's backseat. Today, Easter grass and Santa are on my never-do-again list.

Back to my story. At seventeen, a high school friend of mine kept pestering me to attend a youth group at her church. I finally gave in and joined her. Church and whatever "youth group" offered was the farthest thing from my mind. My family had no interest in God, Jesus, and the only spirits in our home were ghosts. Not the Holy Ghost—tormenting demons living in our closet. Well, you get the idea.

As we entered the back room of her church, there sat sixty-plus teenagers scattered around tables, laughing and sharing stories from the last football game. Since cheerleading interested me, I thought, *Well, maybe these people aren't so bad.* As soon as we sat down, a group of girls came over to our table and introduced themselves. Sue, my friend, obviously knew everyone and held the attention of the boys in the group.

A young man in jeans and a t-shirt, with hair flowing down his back, shuffled past my chair. "Hi, my name is Jim. I'm the youth pastor at this church." He proceeded to talk about some retreat coming up and announcements while my mind bounced around hearing bits and pieces.

Not long after, his focus changed and caught my attention. He spoke of a man who never leaves you, will always love you, and never hurts you. My eyes couldn't leave Jim's; it seemed everyone else had disappeared—like, when you have a dream and it's fuzzy around the edges. How could this be? All of the men in my life abused my mom and me. Over the last seventeen years, I attended seven different schools, lived in countless homes, and the next year would graduate from my second high school. To hear there was a man who would never leave or hurt me pierced my heart.

I remember it as if it happened a minute ago. I jumped up involuntarily, raising my arm in the air. "Who is this man? I want to meet Him." The room chuckled. They knew something I didn't, but it didn't matter what they thought of me, I wanted to know this man! Jim gently explained how Jesus is the person who will never abandon me or hurt me. His words felt like silk pouring over my arms and legs; I could feel something, that thing was the Holy Spirit. I fell to the floor and cried out, "Forgive me, God, I need You!"

The water flowed from my eyes with such force, my face lay on the carpet, soaking it with my tears. I'm not sure when everyone left or their conversations ended.

Jim and Sue sat next to me and led me through a prayer of surrender. For months, I attended church and youth group. The saying, "She is like a sponge soaking up everything," described the end of my teen years. One thing I promised God was that any person with whom I came in contact would choose Him. I'm not the Holy Spirit; I can't make someone believe, but I can tell them the Good News of Jesus Christ and how much He loves them.

I attended baptism, Bible classes, and was discipled by leaders in the church, and they continued until I met a boy from out of town. I made old choices, which led to guilt and shame. One day, while slouched over on my bed, I cried out to God, "Help me! How did I get here? I know You love me, but I have given into my old self and desires."

What never occurred to me was that I had given into the plans of the enemy and listened to his voice instead of God's. I felt dirty, ashamed, and lost. Gazing out my bedroom window, I repeated the prayer: "Help me come back, Father God." Suddenly, a bright light shone through the window like a flash. I heard in my heart—Romans 8:1-2. These were not verses I had memorized or even studied. My Bible was under the bed covered in dust. I grabbed it and turned to the book of Romans. God told me this verse was for me; it would never leave me. Romans 8:1-2 says,

> *"Therefore there is no condemnation for those who are in Christ Jesus,*
> *because through Christ Jesus the law of the Spirit who gives life*
> *has set you free from the law of sin and death."*

As I read it, I remembered the time at the church, lying on the floor sobbing and giving my life to Christ.

God reminded me, "You belong to Me. There is no reason for you to feel ashamed; return to Me and get back on track." Immediately, I knew what to do. I broke off the relationship with the boy and started reading my Bible again.

My life is not perfect. I struggle with different self-doubts, but I know who I am in Christ and no one can take that away from me. If condemnation creeps in, I pray to Jesus, reminding the darkness that Christ's blood covers my sins. I am a child of God, a child of the King! My life differs from what it was, but the enemy still tries to condemn me—staying free is a choice. The Practical Experiments help by giving guidelines in listening to God's voice. To this day, I enjoy listening to God's guidance, and am over the moon thrilled in teaching them to others who long to be free.

Jesus never leaves us—we abandon *Him* by not reading His Word and struggling to do life without Him. Once you accept Jesus died for your sins and believe He is the Son of God, you are His child; He will not let you wander too far. He allows things to happen in your life to draw you back to Him. You can run, but you can't hide, as the saying goes.

Why do I share this with you? Because you are the person about whom I promised God, over forty-five years ago, to share His love and Good News.

God has a verse or set of verses for you. It doesn't have to be a bright light coming through your bedroom window or even happen today, but keep asking and He will lead you to the verses you need for your life.

LET'S GET STARTED.

First, find a quiet place where you and Jesus can connect. You need your journal, Bible, and something to write with.

Next, ask God to help you hear Him clearly. Share with God what you are struggling with and then ask Him the Big Question. *What is the life verse you have for me?* You can also ask for a verse for your children or grandchildren. These make exceptional gifts to share with family members.

Wait and be still; listen. Don't rush this process. It may come the first time you ask, or it might be after several days or weeks. He knows what you lack and when you need your life verse.

Last, when you hear a verse in your mind, write it down and look it up in your Bible. Enjoy your time—everyone's story is extraordinary. I shared mine and I hope one day to hear yours. I am praying for you to hear God everyday throughout the day.

You may think *"This can't happen to me,"* or *"I don't have a testimony that would lead to a life verse."* Let me tell you, everyone has a life verse or verses! God has something special to share with you as His child. And as far as not having a testimony, isn't Jesus enough?

Jesus is your testimony! He is the One who suffered and died for your sins. I wish my childhood had been different and I could say my earthly father loved me, but it's not true. However my Heavenly Father adores me, scars and all. He is the person we brag about, not the gross sins surrounding our past. Are you getting the point? Everyone has a testimony and it's Jesus Christ and His story of love.

In the next chapter, you will need your Bible and journal. Perusing through the Psalms, you will find a whole new way to connect with God.

FOURTEEN

Your Own Personal Psalm

PRACTICAL EXPERIMENT 9

YOU WILL NEED your Bible and journal.

PRACTICAL EXPERIMENT #9

But I can't write!

No worries, I will not leave you without help. Even if you don't love writing, everyone can write something, you'll see.

God gave us Psalms to praise Him, hear His voice, and learn about life. (The word *Psalms* means: songs and poems to be sung with the accompaniment of string instruments.)

David wrote many of the Psalms expressing his every emotion, from depression and loneliness to elated happiness and love. A man after God's own heart. WOW!

Do you sing or hum when you are going throughout the day? If so, keep it up. You might have a psalm in your heart that needs to be shared.

THE PSALMS ARE WRITTEN in five books within 150 chapters.

Book 1 — Psalms 1-41

These emphasize how **God is beside us.**

David writes, "There is no reason to fear any evil because God is always with us."

BOOK 2–PSALMS **42-72**

This shows how **God goes before us** and creates in us a clean heart when we ask Him. This book is full of life-changing advice in surrendering to God daily.

BOOK 3–PSALMS **73-89**

This section reminds us **God is around us.** It emphasizes the history of God's people. God is at work now and has been working since the beginning of time. He spoke to the children of Israel and He speaks to us today.

BOOK 4–PSALMS **90-106**

This book is about how **God is above us**. He is living and reigns forever. While our time on earth is brief, God is eternal.

BOOK 5–PSALMS **107-150**

This is the final book within Psalms. It emphasizes how **God is among us** in our daily life and how we need to have a healthy fear of God to have peace in this thing called life.

WHEN YOU FIND it difficult to praise God, the Psalms is the perfect place to read David's or even Moses's songs of encouragement.

· · ·

PSALMS PRACTICAL EXPERIMENT

Which section of Psalms sounds the most interesting? God beside you, before you, around you, above you, or among you?

Open your Bible to one of the chapters within that section of Psalms. Ask God to show you a specific chapter within the section you are interested in. God uses your interest to guide your heart, so ask Him to ensure you are focused on what He wants to say and not just reading some lines for no reason.

As you read a few verses in the Psalms, ask God to show you something about His character or something from Him personally. Then, step out in faith believing He will speak to you. You don't have to read the entire Psalm, just a few lines here and there. Keep reading until you read a verse that jumps out at you. A line from a psalm that makes you feel something. It could be a favorite one you've read before or a new one with a different understanding.

Spend the next five minutes searching the Psalms. Here is where the fun begins.

#1 Take out your journal.

#2 Write any lines or sections of the Psalms that you read. Either by sitting and being still or strolling around your room, seek God to give you a psalm, one that speaks to your heart.

#3 Start writing! Write as many lines as you like. You can take lines from His Psalms and mix them with several others to create your own, or combine your thoughts from God with His Psalms. There is no wrong way to hear God. As you create your psalm from God, don't worry about spelling or punctuation. Just enjoy hearing from Him and write. If negative thoughts come to your mind, for example, "This is dumb" or "I am not hearing anything" then pause. Go back to #2 and *ask God*. Don't let the enemy win this Practical Experiment.

#4 Finish your psalm. *But, how do I know I'm finished?* When words and ideas end and you feel you need to force it to continue, stop writing. This is about you and God, not how long you write.

. . .

READ YOUR PALMS OUT LOUD. Listen to what God is revealing to you.

You just heard the voice of God! How does it feel? My grown children/grandchildren have been participating in this Practical Experiment for years. They have journals filled with psalms from over the past 20 years. It's exciting to ponder back over them and remember how God gave you your own psalm. What a gift.

Have fun with it. Share your writings with friends or your spouse. The more you experience, the better your mind will start being able to tell when God is speaking to you.

EXAMPLE **of the Psalms Experiment**

Here is an example of one of my sections of a Psalms Experiment.

TAKEN **from Psalms 104:1**

Bless the Lord, O my soul

O Lord my God, you are very great!

You are clothed in splendor and majesty.

TAKEN FROM PSALMS 46:1-2, **10**

God is our refuge and strength, a very present help in trouble.

Therefore, we will not fear, though the earth gives way.

Be still and know that I am God.

TAKEN FROM PSALM 34:13,14

Keep your tongue from evil and your lips from speaking deceit.

Turn away from evil and do good; seek peace and pursue it.

THESE ARE a few sections in various Psalms that I gathered after seeking God to speak to me about a fear with which my friend struggled. I love praising God by reading passages of Scripture like 104:1, which led me to write my personal psalm, which I then shared with my friend. We prayed together and shared how God's Word is faithful in chasing away fear and doubt.

I am not saying we are to rewrite the book of Psalms—or presume we can write anything better than the scriptures. The purpose is to hear God speaking to us personally by asking God, reading His word, writing down verses that speak to us, and then obeying what He says.

Have fun with your Bible. It is a love letter from God to you.

You did it! How does it feel to have completed ten different ways to hear God speak to you?

Great? Amazing? I pray it has been a helpful ten day journey. Don't stop now, read on to make sure you stay connected over a lifetime of listening and obeying God.

FIFTEEN

Staying Connected With God's Voice

PRACTICAL EXPERIMENT 10 AND BEYOND

YOU WILL NEED your new listening-to-God skills and creativity.

PRACTICAL EXPERIMENT #10

You've completed 9 of the 10 experiments! WOW, you are great! The 10th Practical Experiment is for you to ask God for your own personal experience in listening to Him. Maybe while walking your pet? Or doing the dishes? I would love to hear the different ways in which you found listening to your Savior. Submit them to me for a chance to be posted them in our *Get Out Of My Head* private FB group.

So Now what?

You have experienced hearing God's voice, maybe for the first time or this is a normal way of life for you as a follower of Jesus Christ. Great!

Let's not allow this to be a mountaintop experience, but a daily way of listening to the voice of God at home or anywhere you travel. Enjoy sharing these Practical Experiments with your children or grandchildren. Watch the atmosphere at home change when your family starts listening to your Almighty Creator together.

This is a plan of attack to keep your mind free from internal struggles. They are bound to try and return, but now you have the answers by replacing them with knowing God's voice.

READ YOUR PRACTICAL EXPERIMENTS JOURNAL.

Underline the things God shared with you about your life. Maybe promises He reminded you of or verses in the Bible that spoke to you. Special treasures from God.

Circle attitude changes you made—feelings that were not from God, but from the enemy, self-talk, or your peers. Self-talk that has changed.

Put a star on the pages that you will return to for encouragement when life is difficult. These can also be your favorite experiments to encounter again.

Now spend some time praising God for all He has shown you in dealing with internal struggles.

Sing, dance, listen to praise music, however you enjoy praising your Savior, do it!

Ask Him for _more_—more times with Him listening using His Word, clay, chalk, writing letters and psalms. Make up your own experiments. I would love to hear about them. (coniknepper@gmail.com)

These are for you and Jesus to connect as often as time permits. Which leads us into time.

TIME

You have hopefully participated in ten days of time with Jesus.

Keep going by choosing a specific time and place where you can continue with your Practical Experiments. Put this on your calendar, in your phone, and on your personal/business appointments. This is a non negotiable appointment with Jesus Christ Himself. When someone asks for this time just say, "Nope I'm booked, however I can meet you during _____ time of day." The more this becomes a habit, the easier it is to say no to distractions. If you think you are that irreplaceable, then maybe going back and redoing the chapter on pride will help.

Have a plan if you have small children at home. Remember to set yourself up for time with Jesus the night before. YOU CAN DO THIS!

Allow your children to see how important your time is with Jesus. Our daughter has educational programs for her younger children to watch in case they wake up early during her appointment with Jesus. She and her husband take turns in the morning hours to cover the responsibility of their newborn. They honor each other by allowing one to have a listening time with Jesus while the other one takes care of the younger children, then vice versa. They plan ahead and make the time slot. This is not 100% perfect, but even if it works 80% of the time, it's time.

Our three children are grown and in their 40's with their own children. When they're asked, "What did you notice about your parents as a child growing up? How did your parents affect you spiritually?"

The answer is always, "We noticed our dad never gave up his time with Jesus in the morning. The Word of God is a high priority for dad." All three of our children study God's Word on their own and hold it as a high standard in their lives. Who do you think they learned that from? Yep, their earthy father.

Parents, you give the gift to your children of being in the Word and teaching them how to experience listening to God. Telling them He loves them is good news, but leading them into the presence of knowing God's voice, compared to the other voices screaming for their attention, is a life changer for them and you.

GET INVOLVED

Stay involved in your church or start attending one. Seek out other followers of Christ. Join a *Get Out Of My Head* Facebook group.

I pray *Get Out Of My Head* has been helpful for you. You have the tools. I know you can do this. The enemy and your self-talk will press hard on you over the next few days. Go back and read Scripture, choose an experiment to repeat, ask God and HE will help you continue in your freedom.

Please know you can join the *Get Out Of My Head* private Facebook group by emailing me coniknepper@gmail.com. This is a safe place to share victories and struggles in keeping internal struggles out of your head.

Lastly, share this book with a friend and go through it together or with your family as mentioned earlier. The more people learn about the voices hammering for their attention and how to get rid of them, the more people will be able to share the Good News of Jesus Christ, His grace, and live free from tormenting thoughts!

You can purchase books for your Bible Study groups, friends, family members and churches at ConiKnepper.com or anywhere books are sold. You can book a *Get Out Of My Head* workshop or conference by emailing coniknepper@gmail.com.

Again, thank you and Be FREE!

in HIM, Coni Knepper xoxoxo

YOU ARE NO LONGER CONDEMNED, you have been set free from death and all internal struggles!

SIXTEEN

Do I Believe?

THE GOOD NEWS: This is the plan of salvation and grace teachings.

You must first grasp God's grace towards you before understanding the amazing gift of salvation. Read over all the verses and then ask God to speak to you about your relationship with Him, your Heavenly Father. Do you know where you stand with Jesus?

Where I live in Tanzania, East African people believe every time you sin, the Holy Spirit leaves you, which means they believe that when you die, if you have not confessed a sin, then you go to Hell. They do not understand the concept of grace. Grace is what the entire Bible is all about.

> "The law was given through Moses; grace and truth came through Jesus Christ." —John 1:17

> "We believe it is through the grace of our Lord Jesus that we are saved, just as we are." —Acts 15:11

> "Jesus said, 'My grace is sufficient for you, for my power is made perfect in weakness.'" —2 Corinthians 12:9

JESUS CAME to save you from your sins and rebellious behavior. He died for the sins you did yesterday, today, and tomorrow. It is a free gift from God. Jesus's blood is enough. His death brought freedom from casting your soul into Hell and living a miserable life here. Hell is an actual place, but that is another book.

> "In Him (Jesus), we have redemption through His blood, the forgiveness of sins, in accordance with the riches of God's grace." —Ephesians 1:7

> "...made us alive with Christ even when we were dead in our sins—it is by grace you have been saved." —Ephesians 1:5

> "For it is by grace you have been saved, through faith—and this not from yourselves, it is the gift of God." —Ephesians 2:8

GOD'S SPIRIT testifies for us. His Holy Spirit is our seal of approval!

> "And you also were included in Christ when you heard the message of truth, the gospel of your salvation, When you believed, you were marked in him with a seal. The promised Holy Spirit." —Ephesians 1:13

He wants to say amazing things to you through a love letter from Him, the Bible. If you were to die today, do you know where you'd go? If you know the Holy Spirit lives in you, if you have surrendered your life to God and believe Jesus is His Son, then you are saved—period. No one can snatch you out of the hand of God, not even your sins.

> "I give them eternal life, and they shall never perish, no one will snatch them out of my hand. My Father, who has given me (Jesus), is greater than all, no one can snatch

them out of the Father's hand. I and the Father are one."
—John 10:28-30

That is grace. We do not deserve it; we deserve to die and go to Hell, but God had another plan, and that plan is to love us forever *if* we choose to believe in His Son.

"For the grace of God that brings salvation has appeared to all men." —Titus 2:11

Here are some verses in the Bible to better understand how far away from God we have become.

"For all have sinned and fall short of the glory of God."
—Romans 3:23

Meaning, we have all done things against God that are displeasing to Him. There is no one who is innocent. Everyone is a sinner.

"None is righteous, no, not one; no one understands' no one seeks God. All have turned aside; together they have become worthless; no one does good, not even one. Their throat is an open grave; they use their tongues to deceive. Their mouth is full of curses and bitterness. Their feet are swift to shed blood; in their paths are ruin and misery. and the way of peace they have not known. There is no fear of God before their eyes." —Romans 3:10-18

There is a price for living in sin and not listening to God's voice.

"For the wages of sin is death, but the gift of God is eternal life through Jesus Christ our Lord." —Romans 6:23

Because you sin, you are separated from God forever, but God had a plan from the beginning. He knew we would struggle and need a savior.

We are not able to fix the mess of sin in our life. God has the answer; read on.

> "But God demonstrates His own love towards us, while we
>   were still sinners Christ died for us." —Romans 5:8

Christ suffered and died, even though He is the only person who never sinned. Jesus Christ's death paid for our sins. Jesus Christ's resurrection proves God accepted His death as payment for *your* sins.

WHAT DO **I need to do?**

> "If you confess with your mouth Jesus as Lord and believe in
>   your heart that God raised Him from the dead, you will be
>   saved. For everyone who calls on the lord will be
>   saved." —Romans 10:9,13

Because of what Jesus did for you on the cross by dying for your sins, all you have to do is believe in Him and trust His death as payment for your sins. And you will be saved Period! There are no works on your part. Jesus did it all, and it is enough to save you.

> "For it is by grace you have been saved, through faith—and
>   this not from yourselves, it is the gift of God."
> —Ephesians 2:8

Because you chose Jesus as your savior

> "Now you have peace with God and have a relationship with
>   Him." —Romans 5:1

A relationship means sharing back-and-forth, hearing each other communicate. You can hear the voice of God and you can kick other voices out of your head.

You are never condemned again.

"There is no condemnation for those who follow Christ as
their savior." —Romans 8:1

Even if people still speak poorly of you or try to condemn you, Christ never will.

"Nothing can separate you from the love of God."
—Romans 8:38

Not even death. You have nothing to fear in dying if you choose Jesus as your Lord and Savior because He conquered death for you.

If, after reading these verses, you believe that you are a sinner who needs a savior, and that the savior is Jesus...

- If you believe He died for your sins and rose again, conquering death for you...

- If you understand that only your flesh dies and that your soul enters Heaven after this life is over and you will live forever with God in Heaven...

- If you believe there is no other way to God but through Jesus Christ, His Son...

- And if you want to surrender your life to Jesus, then pray a prayer like this:

(Remember, all you do is believe and confess—Jesus has done the rest for you.)

> *Dear Jesus,*
>
> *After reading Your words, I believe You are my only hope. I have sinned.*
>
> *Please forgive me for allowing (fill in your sin) to separate us.*
>
> *I choose today to believe that You, Jesus, are the Son of God. I believe I am a sinner and only You, Jesus, can save me from my sins because You died for me and rose again, conquering death for me.*
>
> *I confess that I have been living for myself in darkness with no way out of my misery.*
>
> *I desire peace with You, Jesus, and choose to give my life to You and follow Your Word. I ask You to fill me with Your Holy Spirit to help me in my new life following You, Jesus.*
>
> *I love You, Jesus. I need You today and always.*
>
> *In the name of Jesus Christ, I pray for these things.*
>
> Amen.

(Which simply means that you agree with what you prayed.)

Take a deep breath—welcome to the family of God!!! Congratulations, you just made the most important decision of your life. Now there is no condemnation, and no one can separate you from Christ and His promises of Heaven for you. God has written your name in the book of life, eternal life with all other believers. Jesus Christ Himself is preparing a place for you.

In the meantime, I encourage you to share with five people how you confessed with your mouth and believe in your heart that Jesus is your Lord and Savior. You need to share the Good News. The enemy and others who do not know Jesus will try to change your mind or give you a hard time. If you hear lies like, "You can't get saved reading a book," or "Those things you read are not true; the author is a crazy lady," or "Your prayer changed nothing; you did it wrong," reject those thoughts! They are all LIES from Satan and confused family or friends. You are saved from your sins. You are a child of God. I promise; it's all real.

Get into the Bible, a group of believers, and ask questions. Keep growing.

Now, go back and try the Practical Experiments. They will mean much more to you as a person being led by the Holy Spirit. The Holy Spirit is the gift God just gave you when you prayed to believe and follow Jesus Christ. When God sees you, He sees His Spirit stamped on your heart, saying, "This is my child." You belong to Him, your new Heavenly Father.

I am so excited to hear how you are doing, what questions you may have, along with helping you get connected with other believers in your area. If you have questions or want to pray together, my contact is coniknepper@gmail.com.

I love to pray, especially with new believers.

God Bless, in HIM, Coni xoxoxo

SEVENTEEN

Extra Helps

HERE IS a link to Freedom In Christ Ministries where you can read the Statement of Faith: www.ficm.org

It is a powerful way to start your day, or proclaim it with your family. There are several free helpful videos and articles about taking control of your mind and staying free.

Philippians 4:8 Poster

Because I Am

In the Name of Jesus
By the power of the Holy Spirit
I choose to NOT
Believe the lies in my head
Because I am...

When negative thoughts or attitudes come.

1. Look at them and take a WIF. Where is it coming from?

Myself, the enemy, my peers, or God?

2. Get rid of the lie. You have the power in you to tell it where to go. *I do NOT give that voice permission to mess with my head!*

3. Replace the lie or attitude with the thoughts of Christ. His love, peace, strength, forgiveness, and truth.

4. Speak out loud the Word of God. Quote Scripture or look them up in your Bible.

5. Praise God!

6. Think about what you think about.

Corrie ten Boom once said:

"Don't pray when you feel like it. Have an appointment with the Lord and keep it. A man is powerful on his knees."

SCRIPTURES to pray and meditate on.

When you don't know what to pray, turning to God for the perfect words brings encouragement, peace, and answers to your struggles.

The next few pages are verses from the Old and New testaments. Verses you can fill in with your name or others you are praying for them. Reading Scripture and asking God what He wants to say to you helps in hearing Him speak. There is nothing wrong with praying your own words, however, there are enormous amounts of power when you pray God's words.

Here are some of my favorite Scriptures to pray through:

Scripture:

> "But those who hope in the Lord will renew their strength.
>   They will soar on wings like eagles; they will run and not
>   grow weary, they will walk and not be faint."
> —Isaiah 40:31

Your prayer can look something like this:

Lord Jesus, I choose to put my hope in You. Thank You for the promise that You will renew my strength. Help me to soar like an eagle today, run and not grow weary with all the things I need to accomplish in this busy day. Lord, I only want to do what You want and with Your strength. Show me how to walk and not be faint in my relationship with You. Help me to hear Your voice. I love You, Jesus. Thank You for life.

Another example of praying God's words.

Scripture:

> "But seek first his kingdom and his righteousness, and all
> these things will be given to you as well." —Matthew 6:33

A possible prayer:

Lord Jesus, I choose to seek You first today and Your will. Help me to listen to Your plans and not my own. Thank You for the promise that when I do this, You will take care of all the things I need for today. I praise You, Lord!

You can also pray this for someone else-

Lord Jesus, I pray for _____, that he/she will seek You first today. Give him/her strength in the decisions _____ needs to make. Father, I thank You that all the things _____ needs are provided for by You, our Heavenly Father. In Jesus's name.

Another example of praying God's Words.-

> "Keep this Book of the Law always on your lips; meditate on it
> day and night, so that you may be careful to do everything
> written in it. Then you will be prosperous and successful."
> —Joshua 1:8

Your possible response to these verses:

Lord Jesus, I need You. Give me the desire to read Your word. Help me today to do what is written in the Bible and not what the world says is right. Thank You for the promise that when I meditate on the scriptures, I will be successful. I choose to set aside _____ minutes today to read Your word and do what You want me to do today. When I speak to someone, let it be full of Your words, not mine. In Jesus's name I ask these things.

A Prayer you can pray word for word from the book of Ephesians 3:14-20:

I pray these Scriptures for our staff or before meetings.

> For this reason, I kneel before the Father, from whom every family in heaven and on earth derives its name. I pray that out of his glorious riches he may strengthen you with power through his Spirit in your inner being, so that Christ may dwell in your hearts through faith. And I pray that you, being rooted and established in love, may have power, together with all the Lord's holy people, to grasp how wide and long and high and deep is the love of Christ, and to know this love that surpasses knowledge — that you may be filled to the measure of all the fullness of God.
> Now to him who is able to do immeasurably more than all we ask or imagine, according to his power that is at work within us, I ask these things in Jesus's Name.

It's your turn. Read through the verses in this chapter and see how you can pray for yourself and others. Jesus is right here with you. Ask for His help and He will give you the desires of your heart. Enjoy! Have Fun!

These are Scriptures I pray for our adult children:

> "And this is my prayer: that your love may abound more and more in knowledge and depth of insight, so that you may be able to discern what is best and may be pure and blameless for the day of Christ, filled with the fruit of righteousness that comes through Jesus Christ — to the glory and praise of God." — Philippians 1:9-11

> "Show me your ways, Lord, teach me your paths. Guide me in your truth and teach me, for you are God my Savior, and my hope is in you all day long. Remember, Lord, your great mercy and love, for they are from of old. Do not remember the sins of my youth and my rebellious ways; according to your love remember me, for you, Lord, are good." — Psalm 25:4-7

Other Books by Coni Knepper

Flip Flop Drip Drop

Gurgle Gurgle Splat

Taka Taka Whoosh!

Little Dude and His Shagalabagala Day

When I Grow Up

Get Out Of My Head

Available where books are sold

and

coniknepper.com

Made in the USA
Middletown, DE
31 May 2022

66431886R00080